MAJOR MODERN AND
CONTEMPORARY THEOLOGIES

MAJOR MODERN AND CONTEMPORARY THEOLOGIES

A Handbook of Digests

Howard A. Slaatté

University Press of America, Inc.
Lanham • New York • London

BT
28
,S54
1997

Copyright © 1997 by
University Press of America, ® Inc.
4720 Boston Way
Lanham, Maryland 20706

3 Henrietta Street
London, WC2E 8LU England

Library of Congress Cataloging-in-Publication Data

Slaatte, Howard, Alexander.
Major modern and contemporary theologies : a handbook of digests /
Howard A. Slaatte.
p.   cm.
Includes bibliographical references.
1. Theology, Doctrinal--History--19th century. 2. Theology,
Doctrinal--History--20th century. I. Title.
BT28.S54 1996   230'.092'2--dc20   96-35447 CIP

ISBN 0-7618-0577-X (pbk: alk. ppr.)

⊖™ The paper used in this publication meets the minimum
requirements of American National Standard for information
Sciences—Permanence of Paper for Printed Library Materials,
ANSI Z39.48—1984

Contents

Foreword

by
Dr. John Goodwin

I have long looked for a concise guide to the principal theological thinkers of this and the preceding century. My friend and former colleague, Howard Slaatte, has now amply met this need with the present volume. One should not be fooled by its size. Professor Slaatte has captured the essence of each thinker's main contribution, "warts and all." His critique of each theologian's stance is balanced and insightful, generous where credit is due, respectful and candid where the author takes issue with a major point. There is no nit-picking here. He asks the proper questions to clarify possible weaknesses or unresolved conflicts. He is completely fair and evenhanded at every turn, with no ax to grind. His grasp of principal issues and their consequences is truly impressive.

This volume will serve as a handy refresher for those who, like myself, studied the works of these theologians in seminary or graduate school. It will also prove accessible to educated lay persons who want to understand the theological issues addressed by these thinkers. Dr. Slaatte does an excellent job of indicating how the work he is discussing relates to traditional Catholic or Protestant thought, as well as possible implications for both right-wing and left-wing positions within those camps.

As the author observes: "Truth is always an encounter . . . Theologians are often slow to see this in the bible. Not a subject-object antithesis on a rational basis, it is an I-Thou relation. Old orthodoxies both Roman and Protestant, objectified it; liberal empiricisms subjectified it. Both are wrong. (No either/or here!)" (p. 71).

Even if you already know where Barth and Brunner agreed and disagreed, and why, you will find this a fresh treatment with new insights and clarifications. Showing an excellent grasp of the main theological writings and currents in the past two hundred years, the author also throws in some "bonus" tidbits. For instance, I never realized (or had forgotten) that Reinhold Niebuhr "borrowed" much of his *Nature and Destiny of Man* (his Gifford Lectures) from Emil Brunner, without bothering to acknowledge that debt. This is not to take away from Niebuhr's genuine creativity in the area of politics and social ethics, which was his forte, but to keep the record straight. Brunner, while overshadowed by Barth in this country, made an enormous contribution to American religious thought, much of it unrecognized, I think. The present volume will also clarify for many the thought of Tillich and Bultmann in a valuable way. This will be especially helpful for those like myself who were trained in theologically conservative schools and heard only negatives about those men. Enjoy. You are in for a treat.

Preface

This book is a condensation of the leading theological schools of thought in the last two centuries. As the title suggests, it consists of summaries or digests of the main ideas perpetrated by the *most creative* theologians of this period.

The aim of the author is to provide students and pastors, as well as teachers, a handy set of studies to keep them alert to the central issues in theology while abreast of the leading movements essential to mature understanding of the issues to which they appertain in theology and churchmanship.

The variety of emphases in this work is enough to convince the reader that the book is not an exposure of a single theme, emphasis or school of thought. Several emphases are included so as to pose dialectical issues, the understanding of which is essential to the reader's own theological shrewdness and maturity. In this respect this short book becomes a study guide even as it is hoped that it will provoke insights important to a current exchange in religious thought. Such an exchange is usually healthful, especially when dogmatic emphases are seen to be a hindrance to a reasonable ecumenicity in the face of current problems in the Church and the world, which need to be addressed or resolved.

This approach by no means is meant to promote the notion that anything goes in theology or, on the other hand, that we do not need an authoritative position to guide the Church. Far from it. Rather, it is meant to help the Christian leader to crystallize and perhaps re-crystallize in his mind what is most germane to a sound theology. Yet such an achievement demands an on-going growth in understanding if we are to be at our best in communicating with the intellectual world without selling out to sheer secularism. This in itself is a dialectical issue, since the alternatives before us are these: to keep theology and secular philosophies alien to each other; to fuse or synthesize theology with philosophy; or to interrelate the two disciplines in a schematism that is more like a vibrant discussion than a final system.

This study covers the high-points of the most noted Christian theologies that have appeared in Europe and America in the past two centuries. In the form of digests, it brings out the basic creative insights of the leading theologians on the scene since 1800. Far from being a one-stream strain of thought these thinkers represent a notable variety of interpretations of theological insights based directly and indirectly on the teachings of the Bible. Preeminently, they reckon with the doctrines of the New Testament as focused on Christ, whom they view, each in his own way, as the foremost revealer and personification of the Word of God.

Most of the theologians represented herein are of Protestant vintage while having rudimentary forms of doctrine reaching back to Augustine and Origen of early centuries while presupposing, if not adapting, some of the insights of Thomas Aquinas even as they differ from him. In various ways they reckon with the most original views of the Reformers Luther and Calvin while endeavoring to make their views of divine Grace and other doctrines more palatable to modern intellectual tastes even as they construct newer types of doctrinal systems for communicative and persuasive purposes.

Some people may begin to wonder why there is so much variety among the leading interpreters of recent generations. Two factors address this matter. First, theologians can be much like artists who see the same things differently and yet endeavor to be true to the distinctive N.T. teachings and emphases. Second, theologians of the post-enlightenment period as well as the twentieth century have seen the need to present theology in ways that prove relevant to the problems and perspectives of the times in which they work. The emphases of the nineteenth century theologians have represented, in the main, a shift from the rationalistic thinking of medieval times to the empirical types akin to the scientific thought of recent centuries. The twentieth century theologians, for the most part, have related this approach to more holistic and existential interpretations, which endeavor to do justice to the full view of man and epistemology while demanding respect for man's concrete individuality. Then, too, some of this century's theologians have opened up respect for social ethics from a spiritual point-of-view.

Fundamental to understanding and appreciating the endeavors of these varied thinkers is the basic issue of likeness and difference not unlike that of oneness and manyness or unity and diversity. Without respect for these principles it would be impossible to classify all or most of the varied thinkers as creatively Christian. Furthermore, it would otherwise be hard to avoid forms of one-sided prejudice. Many Christian interpreters of today might well re-consider how varied types of witness to Christ are not out of order. Jesus even inferred something akin to this when addressing his disciples, for he said, "I have other sheep of other folds (households)." (John 10:16) By the same token we can re-consider the unity in the variety of theological witnessing among the New Testament apostles themselves. Their substance is not extremely different from each other, though their forms of expression are varied. This is because theology, like preaching, must give human thought forms to its divine message. Furthermore, unity and ecumenicity are enhanced when we put the spirit ahead of the letter.

The digests that follow are attempts to epitomize and characterize succinctly the main points of theological insight and methods adopted by the leading theologians of the past two centuries. For dialectical purposes a few criticisms are from time to time included in the discussions. This multi-colored set of summaries should be respected to avoid unnecessary or exclusive partialities. For example, when the author taught systematic theology on the graduate level at Temple University he observed that some students with substantial backgrounds could handle well their own brands of theology, but were weak when it came to treating other brands with intellectual honesty. This, in turn, reflected a deficiency in their dialectical shrewdness as theologians. A basic need in the face of this weakness is sufficient exposure to the variety of emphases in modern and contemporary theology. This book helps meet that need.

This survey is not a cure-all of sorts but an important contribution to both better balanced thinking and more respect for the various types of theology basic to the contemporary frontiers of Christian witness.

Though not heavily documented, this work is directly related to the author's research across the years and his teachings in philosophical theology at Temple University and McMurry University before concentrating on philosophy at Marshall University for many years.

Introduction

The digests of modern and contemporary theologies contained herein are attempts to epitomize the main creative points contended by the leading theologians of the last two centuries. Modern theologies are mainly those of the nineteenth century. Contemporary theologies are largely of the twentieth century.

The modern theologies are varied but highly empirical in emphases or methods. A major 19th Century exception was that of Hans L. Martensen of Denmark whose doctrinal system was based on Hegelian rationalism. As such it became one of the most influential schools after the middle of the 19th century with effectiveness reaching quite popularly into the early decades of the twentieth century. In time it was resisted considerably by the Neo-Reformation theologians under the influence of Søren Kierkegaard's existential philosophy, the pro-Kantian phenomenalism of which led it to resist the rationalism of either the old Scholastic types or the new Hegelian type.

The empirical emphasis in modern theology was inaugurated by Friedrich Schleiermacher of Germany while followed by such theologians as Albrecht Ritschl, Ernst Troeltsch and Adolf von Harnack who gave priority to types of religious experience. Albert Schweitzer capped the movement with an eschatological study of the New Testament related to a critical exegesis of a pro-scientific sort.

At a turning point, after the contemporary theology of the twentieth century was opened up, William Temple of England appeared with a kind of theological bridgehead between modern empiricism in theology and the contemporary neo-Reformation thought which came to a head almost contemporaneously with the work of Temple. Had the neo-orthodox theologians of the continent not become so popular in the early and middle decades of the 20th century, William Temple's theology, as influential as it was, would have had a stronger following.

Karl Barth and Emil Brunner articulated somewhat similar yet distinctive versions of the Neo-Reformed trends in early twentieth century theology. Barth's views were more conservative in the sense that he was further removed from the empirical trends and less sensitive to the place for a religious psychology allowed for by Brunner. Brunner had a stronger respect for *das Anknüpfungspunkt* in man allowing for a spiritual point-of-contact between man and God. Respectful of divine transcendence Brunner viewed it with more anthropological relations than did Barth.

Barth in his earlier years of influence was much in tune with the religious philosophy of Søren Kierkegaard, but eventually pulled away from him to accentuate, rather extremely perhaps, a divine transcendence which in no way had an affinity with human nature or an empirical religious psychology and epistemology, which respected *das Anknüpfungspunkt* in man. Later, Barth relaxed his rigid dualism in favor of the human element as reflected in *Die Menschlichkeit Gottes*.

This problem of the divinely human point of contact becomes one of the basic issues for interpretation in both modern and contemporary theologies as subsequent thinkers wrestle with them.

As a meant-to-be-handy set of studies this series accentuates the distinctiveness of the two newer trends in theology, first the immanental views held by the so-called modern empirical theologians and, second, the more transcendent views in contemporary theology as stressed by the Neo-Reformation thinkers and existential interpreters. In the middle of the 19th century an exception to the empirical emphasis is seen in the Hegelian type of theology held by Hans L. Martensen of Denmark, and in the 20th century an exception is the dual ontological view of William Temple who, almost ahead of his time, correlates metaphysically empirical immanence with doctrinally revealed transcendence. In a sense, then, Temple held to a balanced position which had much in common with both the empirical and the Neo-Reformed points-of-view. Popularly, however, the neo-Reformed theology out-shone Temple's more moderate position, because it was more one-sided in combating almost everything in religion that smacked of empiricism. Being more realistic Temple did not look to such one-sidedness. But it can be asked: Which type of theology is the strongest, the one that is more isolated from empirical thought or the type which embraces it without selling out to it? Dialectically, this issue may be one of the most neglected problems, yet one of the most important, a matter that theological students must keep in mind.

Upon examining this series or set of series, one should not assume that a certain theology builds directly upon another like building blocks of thought. Rather, the pronounced differences between any two or more systems make for dialectical tensions which call for creative comparisons and contrasts even as they tend to pose the cardinal issues in theology. Most of these issues must be reckoned with in the interest of theological shrewdness and maturity of religious thought today. While historical movements are included, this project is not a history of modern and contemporary theology per se. Rather, it poses the types of theologies and movements which have been of marked creativity and consequence in the history of the Christianity of the last two centuries.

Part One

Digests of Modern Theologies

Section I

The Theology of Friedrich Schleiermacher
(1768–1834)

Schleiermacher has been known as the "father of modern liberal theology." This is related to his withdrawal from the long-time rationalistic or Scholastic types of theology made popular in the medieval period and highlighted by Thomism. Associated with the University of Berlin Schleiermacher had a strong background in Moravian pietism while eventually becoming identified with the Reformed Church.

It was Schleiermacher who launched the new era in theology at the beginning of the 19th century by stressing a moral and empirical perspective of Christian soteriology, which was subjective in nature under the influence of pietism. This included a reaction to all rational theology of the post-Reformation period with its scholastic systems and the influences of the 18th century Aufklärung. In this context Schleiermacher saw religion vindicating itself on its own distinctive terms of religious consciousness and experience. Changing ideas in science or philosophy would neither negate nor outdo religious experience, because of its distinctiveness.

Basic to the new movement was Schleiermacher's anthropological approach based on man's inner "feeling of dependence" upon the infinite. As a student aptly described it, this innate capacity amounts to "man's built-in God detector." Later in the century Rudolf Otto of Germany stressed something similar, the "mysterium tremendum" of man's consciousness as set forth in his book *The Idea of the Holy*. This was parallel to Schleiermacher's empirical appeal while emphasizing "the Holy" as the underlying awesomeness of the infinite seen to be basic to religious experience.

This new empirical trend in theology was undergirded by a Kantian respect for moral subjectivity while adapted religiously. Also the movement received some bolstering from the romanticism of philosophers like Schlegel who, too, in his way reacted against classical norms and rationalistic systems. In general the empirical trends promoted profound respect for the individual and his natural pietistic and intuitive outlooks.

Schleiermacher's main work was published in 1800, a book with a strong scientific, empirical approach. Entitled *Addresses on Religion to Its Cultured Despisers,* it was commonly referred to as *Die Reden* or *Addresses.* This was the first attempt to relate theology to a modern Weltanschauung. Basic is the argument for religious feelings. It reflects Schleiermacher's dread of a dichotomy between piety and the intellectual life.

In 1821 Schleiermacher authored another influential work, *The Christian Faith,* reflecting moralistic philosophy as a background for doctrinal theology. Basic are the aids for shaping the self toward a spontaneous moral obedience. (A somewhat reactionary question might be this: But is not the Christian a servant of Christ and not his own authoritative Lord of life?) The book moves into basic Christian doctrines from within the subjective empirical perspective held by Schleiermacher.

In this empirical approach the innate Kantian "ought" is interrelated, if not identified, with the divine Word naturalistically. Giving the individual conscience considerable authority, it tends to lessen the respect for divine transcendence. Functionally, the religious feeling is akin to Kant's "Categorical Imperative" while being more closely allied with the Absolute and not fully identified with the subjective moral element. Feeling and oughtness are viewed as finite human sensitivities, which are related to the awareness of the infinite and universal. Epistemologically, they provide the above mentioned point-of-contact and the near coalescence of divine and human thought.

Metaphysically, for Schleiermacher, God and the world are one immanentally on a moral basis. Feelings are held to precede intuitively both knowledge and will. There is no objective knowledge of God, who is mediated only in this moralistic manner. This immanental scheme is held so strongly by Schleiermacher that Emil Brunner later termed it "semi-pantheistic." Divine will and natural processes are causally identified in the immanental system. Critically, this detracts from the transcendent quality of a free and sovereign God. Transcendence and its redemptive incursions are lost sight of or minimized.

Again, critically, it must be asserted that this anthropocentric view makes the soul the point of departure in religion rather than the revealed Word of God. Most, if not all, empiricisms to follow reflect this tendency to give precedence to religious experience, even priority to the Word in authority. Even Christ is viewed in terms of experience before the doctrinal rudiments centering in "who He is."

Some theologians including those of later existentialist persuasion appreciate how Schleiermacher's pietistic view recovers the place of the biblical "heart" and its relation to a holistic self and a vital religious experience. Dogma is held to be only a subordinate reflection on the experience. Similarly, miracles are "here" and not "there." They have subjective relevance and meaning. Revealed truth becomes a new communication to man about the universe, but its law is not reason or conscience or will but the inner *feeling*. At the turn of the century Rudolf Otto stressed a basic principle quite similar to Schleiermacher's emphasis upon the inner feeling basic to pietism. Otto articulated the inner sense of the awesomeness of the infinite or the sense of *Das Heilige* or "the holy." Central to Otto's expressed philosophy of religion is his book, *The Idea of the Holy*. It is another form of empirical theology based on immanence in religious psychology.

At this point we must recognize the contrast of subjective piety with (a) objective idealism and (b) the existential view of the whole man. As a pietistic perspective this empirical view tends to be independently individualistic.

Later Karl Barth and others regarded this empirical religion as too subjective. It inhibits a real encounter with God who is the Other, not merely one's feelings. Schleiermacher's weak point may very well be his tendency to identify God with man's religious consciousness and its awareness or feeling. In this respect basically he makes all religions to be intuitive in nature, thus giving them a common denominator. This allows Christianity to be superlative only in degree but not in kind.

The strong point of Schleiermacher's theology is that it provides for an awareness of eternal meaning within a temporal becoming. He defends theism differently from the rationalistic view. Defending the person as unique he has a natural theology of moral consciousness, rather than rational argument. As one observes the sublime in life he bows in reverence. On this basis even history has a redemptive element working from within it.

Schleiermacher's position makes a vital contribution to modern thought. He sees the need to determine what Christian religion is empirically before settling for how authoritative and supernatural it may be. This pro-scientific outlook became an important challenge especially to dogmatic fundamentalism. Included here markedly is Schleiermacher's strong regard for what we call "higher criticism" of the Bible, which favors a pro-scientific approach to biblical history, literature and language. This has proven to be a strong contribution to the methods, clarity and communication of theology in the scientific age. Yet it does not succumb to any form of reductionism, for its substance is *sui generic* in view of what science and philosophy commonly deal with. In method it boils down to the application of inductive methods of inquiry before deductive orthodox or rational arguments are concluded. Yet Schleiermacher is concerned more with what men should think and believe now, not merely in the past. Here he is proleptic of an existential principle upon emphasizing the primacy of the present tense of experience and selfhood.

Upon clarifying basic doctrines Schleiermacher's Christology keeps central the union of the divine and the human in one person, but he does not make this a supernatural contention. The virgin birth, for instance, is no guarantee of the divine person. Jesus is a free person, unconstrained even by his divinity, yet not totally free since obeisant to the Father. Schleiermacher anticipates the modern "Jesus of history" emphasis, which developed throughout the century, yet Jesus as the Christ is to him the continuation and completion of man through a superior God-consciousness. His uniqueness is of a moral nature, while having a basic God and man affinity. As such he is a superior "son" spiritually but not the Son as orthodoxy has viewed him metaphysically.

From a neo-Reformed perspective it is held that the Otherness of God and the Word are mitigated by Schleiermacher's subjective approach. Divine objectivity is almost lost. (Problem: Can they be treated rightfully as either without some loss? Barth treats them objectively. Brunner qualifies this. Is it a case of trying to avoid the both/and paradox, which the incarnation bespeaks?)

Schleiermacher saw only legalism among the Old Testament prophets. Here he seems to overlook the revealed God who comes to man. No divine frruption is allowed for. Why? Schleiermacher saw modern cosmology disallowing this and the transcendence implied. Has contemporary theology resolved this issue?

Section II

The Theology of Hans L. Martensen (1808–1884)

Martensen of Denmark was associated with the University of Copenhagen, first as a professor and later as the Lutheran Bishop of Seeland. Upon turning to Martensen there is a sense in which we deliberately interrupt the studies in 19th century empirical theology. This is not only because of Martensen's strong influence upon the thinking of the second half of his century but because his powerful rationalism in theology had to be taken seriously.

This middle-of-the century thinking amounts to a backdrop for modern theology, for it demanded dialectical tussling by the modern theologians who accentuated the empirical perspective as opened up by Schleiermacher and which became popular up to and beyond the turn of the century. The modern theologies then were challenged by the old and yet new types of rationalism even as they had to try to correct the old subservience of theological matters to reason's sufficiency, a matter essential to Martensen's Hegelian rationalism.

Basically, Martensen's system of doctrine or dogmatics was constructed by adapting Hegel's rationalistic dialectics and cosmic System. Yet Hegel's views are tempered wherever Martensen finds them extreme or prone to debilitate orthodox doctrine. Reason is employed consistently upon organizing systematic doctrine with rationalistic support from the cosmic order.

Martensen strongly resisted Schleiermacher's empirical approach as too subjective, while at the same time he resisted the Hegelian threat which tended to reduce the Gospel to philosophy. He saw the need to keep faith primary while maintaining it to be perfectly congruent to reason. Reason, Martensen stressed, was receptive to divine revelation

7

and all findings symmetrical to it. Akin to this, Martensen rejected Kant's skepticism of pure reason in his phenomenalism. Similarly he discounted individualism as seen in pietisms and empirical religion. Here his contemporary Søren Kierkegaard, also of Denmark, differed notably in his holistic existentialism, the epistemology of which is not so delimited.

Martensen's leading work is his *Christian Dogmatics* of 1849, which was used for over two generations as a strong systematics in the Hegelian era. Basic Christian doctrines were made to blend with the Hegelian rationalism with its universal laws and the teleological view of nature. Sacred history was deemed to be within profane history i.e. *Heilsgeschichte* and *Historie* were not at odds. Here Hegel's view of history was seen to blend with revealed thought. Representing the unity of God and man in the world the incarnate Christ was held to be a miracle. Even nature seeks Grace.

Martensen viewed divine transcendence as superior to natural immanence as a disturbance of history and nature by God's will. But what seems miracle to men is "natural to God," said Martensen. (Problem: Is it really miracle, then, on such a rationalistic premise?)

Grace, to Martensen, is elective but not irresistible. This is much like the Arminian view of the Wesleyans, allowing for a free relationship under God's initiative. But faith, is evoked largely by reason's acceptance of evangelical doctrines and the systematics surrounding them. Though there is no disjunction between reason and faith, faith is essential as a trustful means to the higher, revealed truth. Influenced by the Aufklärung, Martensen tends to observe any discontinuity between reason and faith in favor of continuity. This becomes an accommodation to a Hegelian form of theology. Faith is hardly what Kierkegaard referred to as a "leap," nor is sin a serious estrangement affecting reason and man in general.

But in his book *Kristlige Etik* Martensen, under criticism, eventually conceded that Kierkegaard's individualistic view could not be rejected, and "without it pantheism had conquered, unconditionally." This was a tremendous concession to Søren Kierkegaard, for by it Martensen almost topples his strong rationalistic system, for sin and finitude demand more than a basically immanental answer, and a rationalistic structure is rendered suspect.

Section III

The Theology of Albrecht Ritschl (1822–1889)

Later in the last century Ritschl, a Lutheran of the University of Göttingen, followed through on organizing empirical theology. He preferred that Christianity be built on an appraisal of religious events. This subordinated rationalistic speculations and theories to an empirical appraisal of spiritual occurrences. Basic to him was the appeal to the historical Jesus surrounded by "moral values" calling for "value judgments." Faith, then, for Ritschl amounted to the judgment of the values reflected in Jesus and his teachings. Faith was one's appraisal and commitment to what is historically revealed in "the Jesus of history."

Ritschl's position allowed for an individualistic faith and religious knowledge. Such empirical knowledge, however, is not the same as scientific knowledge since conditioned by the interests of the soul. Only a latent existential problem and perspective, it remains a duality of reason and faith.

Ritschl's main work was his *Justification And Reconciliation* published in 1870. This was a book against a subjective pietistic type of empiricism even as it was against objective dogmatics and rationalistic systems. Basic to Christian theology, he believed, was a historically perceived revelation of God in Christ. In this respect Ritschl attacked Schleiermacher's subjectivism. Yet he saw Jesus' incarnation as a value judgment of faith, hence not objective but subjective. The primary appeal is to the historical person and his superior ethics. So in the man Jesus the believer discerns the Lord. This Christology concedes a tension between predicates of Godhood and manhood. Christ's divinity is not based on what is deemed miraculous but upon Jesus' values and their influence within history. As such divinity is not solely susceptible to an empirical perspective but is a value judgment of faith.

Being empirical in a different way, Ritschl differs from Schleiermacher in asserting that doctrines are "givens," which are more than descriptions of religious experience. His historical appeal is used to counter the emphasis upon subjective feelings. Faith rather sees Christ as the revealer of God the Father through historical events. (Problem: But did all men see the Father in him from their historical vantage points?)

Ritschl prefers historical objectivity, but it is seen to be undercut by mystical pietism and a related natural theology. Yet the old rationalistic types of theology are seen to be too extraneous; for instance, the Supreme Being does not forgive or love. But this is perceived by men of history whose faith is also historical. Furthermore, God is known only by a mediated revelation in history.

Ritschl held mysticism to be too unhistorical, for it neglects faith as the basis of love even as it minimizes any form of spiritual mediation. Yet Ritschl tends to overlook the mysticisms of Paul and John in this attack. His basic appeal is to the historical Gospel rather than to reason or religious consciousness. Dogmatics asserts a norm, since by "value judgments" God lays claims upon men. This type of empiricism in theology is based upon a historical appeal which is closer to objective phenomena providing a more authoritative norm. Hence, Ritschl has an empirical appeal that is more pro-scientific than Schleiermacher's view.

Also, Ritschl sees human will and related moral factors preceding knowledge in experience, a matter akin to the epistemology of the existentialists Kierkegaard and Berdyaev. In addition, Ritschl views worth or value judgment as vindicating religious experience, since revelation as related to them does much to resolve the tensions between man and nature. Here we note a pragmatic appeal with God being the support for ethics. Ethical values become primary in religious faith and experience, and the New Testament doctrine of the Kingdom is deemed primarily a set of moral relationships. Empirically, this helps promote good culture, since the Kingdom is God's realm of moral ends for fostering unity through love. But the transcendent element in New Testament teachings and eschatology is lost sight of in Ritschl's empiricism.

Symbolically, Ritschl stresses an ellipse, which has two foci in his scheme. One is the moral kingdom and its principles. The other is the spiritual redemption in Christ. The two, while distinguishable, are in apposition, so that the Kingdom relates the two in reciprocal moral action. Doctrinally, justification and reconciliation express the bi-polar view of soteriology in the unity of the Spirit as acts of God linked with history but not reducible to historical processes per se. In this regard the Church as the steward of God's Word is progressively realizing the Kingdom of God on earth. Justification by faith inspires responsibility for deeds of reconciliation. Justification is a Pauline doctrine which is made vivid through the faith community or church. It is much inspired by Christ's atonement. Here Ritschl may be seen to begin with the earthly Jesus of history who lacks omnipotence yet is deemed pre-existent and honored as Son of God by men's faith judgment. As expressed in the Epistle to the Hebrews he is both prophet and priest, the one is man to God, the other is God to man, as Ritschl puts it.

Though the doctrine of the Trinity was embraced by Ritschl, he was prone to minimize, if not neglect, the Holy Spirit in a "this worldly" approach. Sin was held to be only rebellion by man against God, whereas to God sin is ignorance, said Ritschl. The orthodox doctrine of original sin was disregarded in favor of a stress upon ethical idealism and human strengths and weaknesses in its light. The holy judgment of God was played down. Here Ritschl failed to cope with either existential paradox or despair. His picture of religious men was quite optimistic, for they could live sinlessly quite easily, a trend of thought which pietism sometimes may have catered to. Ritschl's treatise on Christian perfection was written with this optimistic slant.

As for the doctrine of the atonement Ritschl said the fact that Jesus suffered and *died* is historical in nature. But that he died *for me* is a value judgment of faith. Thus revelation is historically objective while faith is the link between the objective events and their subjective relevance. There is a latent existential perspective here but without an emphasis upon a divine-human encounter. Faith's value judgment is more or less on its own as a moral decision with minimal dependence upon the Holy Spirit's inspiration and the confrontation of the Word. The objective element is not transcendent, so any incursion of the divine is played down. Religion rests on historically immanent facts and events, revelation being from within history. (Cf. Hegel and Schleiermacher.) So a different kind of empiricism is catered to by Ritschl with more of a historically scientific reference than found in Schleiermacher's subjective empiricism. In this way Ritschl took man back to the New Testament period as viewed through the Reformation's re-appraisal of Christ and the evangelical doctrines giving witness thereto.

Critically speaking, Ritschl has too simple a continuity between history and revelation. It is true that Christ is *in* history, but he is not altogether *of* it. Jesus had said, "My Kingdom is not of this world." (John 18:36) Being transcendent as well as immanent, eternal as well as temporal, God is incognito to some extent. God in Christ should mean a divine marvel, not a mere factual event of history.

Similarly, in the Ritschlian perspective history can heal its own weaknesses by applying Jesus' ethics on a moral basis. Here immanence is stressed if not over-stressed historically under Hegelian influence. Revealed truth is not deemed an *ekstasis* of an Other from a qualitatively different realm. This dissolves all conceptual tension between time and eternity as a moralistic historical positivism is given its way. This reduces all religion to total immanence, so that there is no distinction between the religion that is universal and the religion of the Mediator. In short the Kingdom of God lacks eschatological transcendence as basic to a teleological fulfillment. It is only a superior ethical activity of "building the Kingdom," which amounts to a form of idealism expressed in history. The redemptive factor is neglected in favor of the moralistic. Not all wrong, it is seriously lacking in a divine inspiration that looks redemptively to a transcendent spirit and quality. The Neo-reformed theologies saw this and the need for a conspicuously revamped approach.

Section IV

The Theology of Ernst Troeltsch (1865–1923)

An empirical theologian with backgrounds in theology at Heidelberg University and in philosophy at the University of Berlin, Troeltsch was influenced by Ritschl and became a theologian of the so-called "religio-historical school." Less of a specialist in dogmatics Troeltsch became more of a historico-social scientist of religion, a fairly new field of studies in his day. His most noted works are the following: *Die Absolutheit des Christentums,* 1909, and *Social Teachings of the Christian Churches.* Also a noted essay on "Historiography" in Hasting's *Encyclopedia.*

Basically, Troeltsch was anxious to interrelate Christianity and culture through an emphasis upon social consciousness as inspired by man's natural religious sensitivity. For him the Kingdom of God can be approximated on earth; being within man it is relatively attainable. Troeltsch had observed that Ritschl had neglected the more objective scientific approach while negating the philosophical perspective in favor of the historical. It was Troeltsch who opened the door to the scientific studies of religions while viewing history as too remote and changing to afford an adequate understanding of revelation. Quite as for Schleiermacher the basic ground for theology must be found elsewhere. Troeltsch believed he had found it in a mystical a-priori or intuition of feeling. This became for him the common denominator of all religions. Akin to this, Troeltsch did much in comparative religion, a pro-scientific field ignored by Ritschl.

This more objective empirical view led Troeltsch to claim that Christianity was syncretistic, its thoughts coming from various ancient ethnic religions. Troeltsch became a systematician of this kind of study and even claimed that New Testament symbols were borrowed and adapted from other religions, the most extensive of such phenomena being expressed in the Book of Revelation. There arose a tendency to assume that these similarities almost determine the Christian faith. So for Troeltsch Christianity amounts to the culmination of various views of revelation and redemption already at work in the past societies. Consequently, Troeltsch views Christianity as a type of general revelation rather than a special revelation. Later, in the early twentieth century the neo-Reformers reversed this emphasis.

Despite his strong objective empiricism Troeltsch was well aware of the dangers of reconciling religion to the near dictation of science and the trends of culture. Also, though religion can use philosophy, it cannot be based upon it. The religious ideas often embraced by philosophy stem from the great historical religions. Here Schleiermacher had much to offer, thought Troeltsch, for he was basically correct in his empirical approach, though incomplete about the scientific perspective of historical religions. This outlook was favorable to a fusion or near fusion of religious empiricism and idealism. The doctrinal standards of value could be retained despite the historical relativisms involved together with the mystical psychologies.

As for Troeltsch's philosophy of history, he saw the real to be the rational in the orders of the universe, a matter related to Hegel's System. As such history is a natural process while also the progressive revelation of God's thought, but, unlike Hegel, Troeltsch saw that we cannot conceive of the Absolute rationally. A different type of religious idealist, he saw the Absolute as God revealing himself and transforming himself from within nature and history, which also gives locus to the conflict of the spirit and the flesh. In this somewhat neo-Platonic monism evil has a metaphysical relation to human nature while being perennially resolved in the future.

In general Troeltsch attempts to harmonize the Christian God with the idealists' philosophy of Spirit. On this basis history, culture, philosophy and religion are aspects of one cosmic whole. A Hegelian unity is basic but not so much as a unity based on a cosmic Reason but a natural uniformity. The religious strength of this position is that spiritually a person is confronted by something distinctive but which reason cannot penetrate either metaphysically or scientifically, though they imply legitimate methods of study. Not favorable to a dualism of reason and faith similar to Ritschl's scheme, Troeltsch is against a supernaturalism in favor of a Hegelian unity and cosmic uniformity. Dogmatics is a matter of practical theology based on the historical and scientific approach while focused on the prophets, Jesus and the Bible. This makes theology of present significance, not something positively fixed, static or unchanging. It is not so much a system or static set of norms but a working guide for life. This has much in common with Schleiermacher.

On this basis Troeltsch tends to obscure a special revelation in favor of man's natural inner religious sensitivity. The Act of God as the special revealer is obscured or dulled. What is deemed to be revelation is but the empirically objective perspective of the subjective intuitive essence of religion. While not the exclusive revelation Christianity is the superlative revelation. Revelation is the interior nature of religion, though it can be studied empirically, even comparatively. This view sees it as immanental and universal, lacking genuine transcendence, since it implies that God is the *ground* of the world, but not its Lord. Later, Tillich, adapts this principle from Troeltsch. Historical research of a somewhat anthropological type actually yields information insuring the scholar of not only origins of and about religion but of norms and hopes. All history is the same, hence amenable to the historical methods involving criticism, analogy and relativistic phenomena.

As for such major Christian doctrines as the Incarnation and Resurrection of Christ Troeltsch sees them as religious poetry unrelated to history objectively; they are symbols of the Unseen. Incarnation and atonement were mythical ideas already in the world and baptized for the Christian purpose of evangelism. As such they convey special meanings for men of faith; their significance is subjective more than objective.

What, then, happens to the missionary outlook? The attitude of Troeltsch is that we are not to convert so much as to educate. God is already at work; He precedes our witness. This empirical view is immanental and tends to detract from the uniqueness of the Gospel. As the Absolute God is felt everywhere and God is universally "transparent" since all of creation is Divine. Only a general revelation is seen through this, there being no special or once-for-all unveiling of something distinctive. Likewise there is nothing supernatural about Christianity's past. (Problem: If there is no unique moment or event that is part of the universal Whole, we have no real clue to its meaning.) Troeltsch's empirical approach yields an intellectual achievement of sorts, whereas the New Testament gives us a faith-conditioned gift and relationship.

Troeltsch does not link the person of Jesus with a principle of redemption in a special divine Act, since he sees all history as relative.

Jesus is a symbol of the eternal, but he is not the Eternal. Similar to the later American theologian Hugh Ross Mackintosh, the claim is that Jesus is the prototype of the faith community. The Divine Love, which he attests, is an "energy," so-called, which naturally fosters union between the finite and the infinite. In this context there is no absolute Christian ethics, so Utopian ideals are dismissed and the Kingdom of God is only approximated in time.

What about immortality? Immortality is merely a return of the human spirit to the timeless (sic) or the universal Divine. This amounts to a Neo-Platonic "absorption." Since Christianity preserves historical individuality, we must ask: What happens to it in death? Unlike the later neo-Reformed thinkers, Troeltsch fails to see that the resurrection is no less than a preserved individuality. Yet he retains the view that the immortal life beyond inspires our temporal, historical life. But is the immortality referred to by Troeltsch only a neo-Platonic absorption, which blots out the individual spirit like the drop of water which is dissolved by the sea? It appears so, any type of selfhood appears to be lost or negated in the cosmic absorption. (Problem: Is not this more like Greek metaphysics than New Testament doctrine?)

All in all Troeltsch holds to a non-skeptical relativism, which caters to the scientific historical method of interpretation of religion as empirical, yet it is linked with a close-to-pantheistic monism. At bottom this tendency is due to man's subjective affinity with the Divine process and God unveiling himself immanentally from within nature and history. While not a perfect fusion in a monistic system nature and spirit retain a tension and struggle intrinsic to both life and religion. The Church is not held to be an extension of the mind of Christ. Rather, in his neo-Platonic system Troeltsch sees a dualism of sorts within the immanental whole, reflected in the clash between historical standards of truth and values. Thus Troeltsch refuses to limit the Platonic principle of Eros or self-gratification to a natural cause and to attribute Christian Agape or sacrificial love to something transcendent; both belong to the one whole system of nature and history.

Troeltsch believes that the Divine manifests itself in new forms of individuality within history. It moves not toward complete unity or universality so much as to the fulfillment of the highest potentialities of each person, each life and every phenomenon. Thus Christianity is not a historical reconciliation so much as a historical individuality. Apologetics which appeal to miracles are dismissed. The universal validity of Christianity is not proved, but it is believed and confirmed by its ability to solve problems and manifest God through the lives of the prophets and in the hearts and lives of men. Ritschl would support this. The Gospel must bring to the world "a new peace and a new brotherhood." This is not to be viewed as universality but as a pluralistic individuality, not as a naturalistic oneness but as a spiritual brotherhood based on ethical commitments. (Problem: What makes for brotherhood amidst a strong individuality? Can it be anything less than a regeneration of spirits under the Spirit of God in Christ making for a Koinonia?)

Critically, it appears that Troeltsch is a strong exponent of what to many others is called "modernism," an empirical view of man's religiosity which neglects or fails to see the importance of regeneration as more than symbolic. This is related, in turn, to a minimal regard for the problem of sin even as it reduces spiritual hope to an optimism about human nature.

Section V

The Theology of Adolf Von Harnack (1851–1930)

Von Harnack was another Lutheran empiricist who specialized in church history and was associated with the schools at Marburg and Berlin. In a broad sense he was quite Ritschlian and stressed the "Jesus of history" together with the "simple Gospel" based on Jesus' teachings as distinct from the "Christ of dogma" as he saw it. Harnack's most important works were these: *What Is Christianity?* (1900), *The History of Dogma* (several volumes), *Christianity and History* and *Marcion*.

Von Harnack saw early Christianity identified with a Hellenized theology "secularized" in the early ecumenical creeds. He interpreted the Gospel of Jesus as based upon (a) the Father and not the Son, (b) the divine sonship of man (all men), and (c) the infinite value of the human soul. Much like Ritschl's position, Harnack dismissed all speculative theology, especially that of Hegelian rationalism. He allowed a dread of metaphysical contentions to extend to the entire transcendent side of the New Testament faith. This led to a reduction of the Gospel to another spiritualized moralism with an idealistic picture of Jesus for men to admire and seek to emulate. As the Word-bearer Jesus was a prophet who gives men the Gospel but who is not of it. Harnack, then, has little place for "the Word made flesh." Rather, Jesus is solely the exemplary teacher and son of man or ideal child of God.

It was the Apostle Paul, thinks Harnack, who welcomed Hellenistic thinking and led to its being blended metaphysically with the simple Gospel of Jesus. This also favored Roman legalism and eventually Western imperialism, Harnack maintained quite extremely. In time the

Protestant Reformation housecleaned this accommodation, and liberal Protestantism, linked with the empirical perspectives, completed the task, thinks Harnack, by its return to the simple religion of Jesus and the eradication of foreign thought. Hence, the central idea of Christianity is love, which is the key to Jesus' ethics. Anders Nygren, a noted Swedish theologian of the mid 20th century, declared Harnack to be wrong, for he stresses the Greek concept of Eros (self-gratifying love) rather than Agápe, the sacrificial love emphasized by both John and Paul in the New Testament. Eros is a form of the pursuit of the value of its object. This is a Platonic aspiration of a moral ideal rather than an expression of an expendable self-giving to others.

Yet Harnack sees the Kingdom of God focused on the inner spiritual growth of persons as based on expressions of love. Though not the same as historical progress, this bespeaks an evolutionary growth, which subordinates the eschatological view since closer to a morally teleological interpretation. Harnack sees a link between experience and the reality of moral and spiritual values, quite like Ritschl.

Harnack goes so far as to say, "Dogma is . . . a product of the Greek spirit in the soil of the Gospel." Gnostic thinking is the acute form thereof and orthodoxy a gradual dilution of it. Both movements betray the religion of the Father to Hellenic thought. The substance is coerced by the form. While stressing the historic pole this amounts to a Kantian dualism of Christ very much in contrast to the neo-Reformed view of the early to mid-twentieth century, which stressed divine transcendence. The Hegelians are held by Harnack to be in error who regarded dogma as merely the necessary unfolding of the faith content from experience. Meaning is from a "supernatural" source, but it is not at odds with history. The Jesus of history is the vehicle of the message of the Kingdom of love. So Harnack declares that we do not need the risen Lord and the judge of history even working from within it.

Harnack retains the spiritual individualism of Ritschl and Troeltsch to the point of minimizing the role of the church. Not only causal in nature, history is a series of the personal effects, and for Christianity faith commitments are understood to be coming out of the past. The present has no significance except as fed by the past. (This depreciates the primacy of the present as stressed by the existentialists). The rationalists are in error for lauding the cosmically objective God of reason and subduing what is spiritually at work in history. Problem: Would Harnack similarly claim the same of the God of transcendence with reference to existentialists from Kierkegaard to Bultmann, who do not give primacy to the role of history?

Harnack has some disdain for Lessing's 18th century view that history is "accidental" and never a proof of the truths of reason as in rationalism. Rather, history is a combination of thought and action akin to Kant's phenomenalistic epistemology. Particulars must not be dissolved or ignored or swallowed up in the Hegelian dialectic. All determinism including that of the latter is rejected in favor of historical persons and events. They are what yield the "effects" in history; therefore they are not "accidental." The spiritual element guides or steers them in history. This demands a dual perspective of history, viz. the objective data and the subjective spiritual interpretation thereof. (Bultmann says the reverse, the latter being basic.) Time as a matter of history (chronos) is a means to the higher spiritual end, so religion relates life to eternal principles, and faith yields a supra-empirical or trans-scientific meaning to history. Being from within history this plays down any transcendent incursion or encounter; it is strictly immanental, i.e. *Historie* but not *Heilsgeschichte*).

In this context Jesus is the Christ or the highest seat of meaning in history understood as an objective historical phenomenon together with his Gospel. The Gospel is the historical expression of the true "community." The faith community looking to this is evidence of the historical Christ, who is the "link" and "indissoluble unity," says Harnack, of history and eternity. Being an immanental interpretation this fails to respect what the existentialists and Neo-Reformed thinkers later have special respect for, viz the qualitative superiority of eternity as transcendent over time. Harnack simply sees history as time absorbed by eternity or merely the on-going process of time or the everlasting continuity of *chronos*. But, if so, eternity is still time. The regenerating or transcendent dimension of eternity is lost sight of here. The history of Jesus or the historical Jesus was not uncommon time for Harnack, since he was limited by his manhood and temporal circumstances. Harnack carries this immanental empirical view so far as to deny miracles to Jesus' ministry. Furthermore, Jesus did not claim to be the Messiah or a divine Son. Though not the Son, Jesus, says Harnack, was one son who *knew* the Father.

In this light Harnack regards the New Testament records as the defense of the believer's faith. The doctrines of the Virgin Birth and the Resurrection are narratives which attempt to attest to or "prove" Christ's divinity, but they lack objective bases. The resurrection, for instance, is a faith datum, not an objective fact. It is a poetic type of witness to Christ's victory over death assuring men's hearts of eternal life and divine love's victory over sin. (Cf. Harnack, *The History of*

Dogma, Vol. I for particulars.) Here we see a similarity to Ritschl's "value judgments," since the subjective relevance of Christ to the person of faith is basic and without which no New Testament would have been written. The redemptive or saving work of Jesus was to solicit men to accept God's love, that they might worship him and obey his command. Jesus had a unique fellowship and knowledge of the Father even as he had a special mission to communicate its basis. Only in that sense was he a mediator.

Harnack denies the divine nature of Christ as well as the atonement. He says that St. Paul began both doctrines when he said, "God was in Christ." These ideas are dogma, says Harnack, but remain historically unprovable. Note: Critically, the later neo-orthodox or neo-Reformed thinkers have a contrasting claim that it is the historical Jesus who is unprovable. Barth, Brunner and Bultmann spearhead this view in favor of a transcendent Christology. But Harnack detests transcendence as attributed to Christ asserting it to be extraneous to men of common history including Jesus. So, as far as Harnack is theologically concerned, Christ saves men solely by his moral appeal in his teachings. This view has a little in common with that of Hastings Rashdall who held to a "moral influence theory" of the atonement, which, too, stresses history and moral appeal.

Harnack maintained that early Greek converts to Christianity were influenced by the identification of Christ with the Logos. He appreciates this as representative of the principle of eternity in history giving status to history as a cosmologically realized ideal. This replaces the incarnation of the eternal and favors the immanental appeal to history.

In general Harnack's position is akin to a dualism that is not metaphysical but ethical, that of the spirit and the flesh. Spiritual sonship is a matter of ethical response. The dualism involved is immanentally perceived quite as it was by Troeltsch. True manhood in history is a principle of eternal value, and the ideal is the real. The reality of history lies in this embodiment of the ideal as the "timeless," as Harnack thinks of it, while pervading the media of history. In this respect the Hegelian type of an Ideal of Reason is replaced by the Ideal of Love. Historically, again, what Jesus did and how he did it were much more important than "Who He Is." In this light all men are called to emulate him as sons of the Father, whatever the metaphysical implications. Focused on the acting Jesus of history the Gospel restores communion between men and the Father. Sin enslaves men to their lower nature and nature in general, whereas love is basic to fulfilled personalities and to community. Institutions, however, tend to compete with this, being too impersonal. Here Harnack reminds us of Rousseau who blamed institutions even before individuals for the corruption of society, however, Harnack believed the Church should appeal to individuals according to the way God rules and show the ethical implications of practical and social affairs. At this point Harnack anticipates the forthcoming "social gospel" which is a "social active principle."

Though Harnack's social ethics looks toward future fulfillment it neglects the fulfilled *eschaton*. Only common history is real, though enriched by activated love. Any form of divine intervention, Harnack says radically, is only escapism. (Contrast the *ekstasis* of Kierkegaard and especially Nicholas Berdyaev.) New Testament eschatology to Harnack is only a persuasive homiletical type of appeal; it is too futuristic, he thinks, so Harnack offsets it with emphasis upon the Johanine present tense Kingdom among individuals under the way God rules. Much like the view of Troeltsch, immortality and the timeless values are being realized here and now, the ultimate aspect thereof belonging to a kind of neo-Platonic absorption into the eternal. Also, much like Troeltsch, Harnack sees two poles or foci of the Kingdom: the future event of fulfillment and the inwardly present workings thereof. Yet he disallows a both/and paradox for doctrinal interpretation.

This empirical, immanental and historical appeal by Harnack is much in contrast to the 20th century emphasis upon "the Christ of faith," as recovered by Martin Kahler, Karl Barth, Emil Brunner, Rudolf Bultmann and Friedrich Gogarten on the continent. Problem: But is it possible these neo-Reformed thinkers have reacted to the extreme right, i.e. an overly strong emphasis upon transcendence? If so, why or how? Can they be appreciated and yet qualified dialectically? (And) can Harnack's strong points be retained without allowing for a historical reductionism? Also, can he be dismissed? The writer addresses these types of issues in his work, *The Paradox of Existentialist Theology.*

A provocative appraisal worth discussing over the dinner table was submitted by George Tyrell some time ago: "The Christ that Harnack sees, looking back . . . is only the reflection of a Liberal Protestant face, seen at the bottom of a deep well." (from *Christianity at the Crossroads*.)

Part Two

Digests of Contemporary Theologies

Section VI

The Theology of Albert Schweitzer (1875–1965)

Albert Schweitzer, whose background was in Alsace, became a Strasbourg New Testament scholar and specialist in philosophy. He had an extensive missionary career in French Equatorial Africa. His thought represented a turning point in theology mainly due to his New Testament eschatology, which was linked with a recovery in critical New Testament studies.

Schweitzer reacted to the German liberalism of the previous emperical schools as centered in the historical Jesus. Their pro-scientific, critical approach, he believed, led to the neglect of the supra-rational elements of the New Testament in favor of the Kingdom-building ethics of Jesus, the teacher. Yet Schweitzer speaks of this Jesus of history as not the Christ of dogma and not intrinsic to the Gospel per se. Even so he concedes the mystical Christ who is more than a man of history.

Schweitzer hit the liberals hardest when he showed that eschatology was basic to Jesus' mission and his teachings of the Kingdom. In view thereof he pointed out that eschatology must not be ignored. Jesus, he said, taught in keeping with current eschatological thought forms, and his message included such issues as the following: (a) The Kingdom is to come or be fulfilled soon in a supernatural way, as implied in Matthew, Chapter 10. Jesus was disappointed when the Kingdom did not come. (b) Jesus was conscious of his Messianic role. (c) The delay of the Kingdom induced Jesus to die for his followers and bring in the Kingdom, hence Jesus did what induced men to crucify him that his coming as the Son of Man in his Kingdom would come to pass.

Noteworthy here is the thought that the Kingdom was more than immanental, yet in what sense it is transcendent is left indefinite in Schweitzer's view. It must be asked: Why the ethical teachings in

Jesus' ministry if a supernatural Kingdom was soon to come about? Schweitzer regards them to be "interim ethics" for Jesus' followers to apply to show that they are of the Kingdom or committed to it. Their belonging to the "interim" implies that they will not be needed when the Kingdom does come to pass. But since the Kingdom is not yet come the ethical teachings are valid for fostering its coming while believers are in the interim.

Liberal critics of the modern emperical perspectives declare that Schweitzer destroys faith in Jesus. Schweitzer so much as replies that the 19th century pictures of the historical Jesus are unreal, so he has restored Jesus to his place as King. Thus, the historical man Jesus is not as "compelling" as is the Messiah-Christ and the divine Son who is known mystically by faith and willful commitment. This pro-mystical position is conceded near the end of Schweitzer's greatest work, *The Quest of the Historical Jesus*.

The approach taken by Schweitzer had pro-scientific elements which contributed to his type of literary "form criticism" or what was originally termed "Formgeschichte" by the German scholars of the last half or so of the 19th century. Schweitzer used this tool to help bring focus back to Jesus' eschatology rather than keep it either peripheral or unreal as the emperical liberals were prone to do. This helped lead scholars to a new study of the tradition in which Jesus had found himself. This form criticism perspective did much to promote respect for the later emphasis of Rudolf Bultmann, who had an existentialist view of Heilsgeschichte and New Testament eschatology.

Noteworthy is the futuristic emphasis in Schweitzer's eschatology. This is much in contrast to Harnack's view as well as the "realized eschatology" of C. H. Dodd with its stress upon the present tense of the Kingdom and redemption as supported by the Fourth Gospel. Can the respective emphases upon the future and the present both be right or wrong? Does the existential perspective have anything to offer here? We must assert that it does when justice is done to the eschato-logical views of both Kierkegaard and Nicholas Berdyaev. The both/ and paradox proves highly relevant here. (Cf. the writer's work *Time And Its End* and *The Paradox of Existentialist Theology*.

Schweitzer boldly asserts that the liberals are in error to "spiritual-ize" the Messianic expectation and neglect its realistic elements in-cluding the expected tribulation of the faithful. Schweitzer regards Harnack's view of things to be the "most modernized theory about Jesus." Like previous emperical interpretations, it spiritualizes the realistic Messianism in favor of an ethical Kingdom for which Jesus

4

died to bring it to victory. Schweitzer, however, sees this as believing in an eschatological end of this world and the related coming of the Son of Man. He did not hesitate to declare that the modern liberals of the empirical schools were wrong, who claimed that the New Testament passages on eschatology are erroneous since unhistorical and rationally unintelligible. To Schweitzer Jesus' love ethic is intensified by a speedy end of the world.

Schweitzer held that working "in the spirit" of the Kingdom is closer to being right than merely "serving" the Kingdom. The latter is usually too temporal a view, so we must reject the 'success' of the world, which is really coming to an end (finis). Jesus put the Spirit first and claimed authority over those who take him and his teachings seriously. Significant is the fact that Schweitzer did not identify the Kingdom with this historical world. At this point he was much in contrast to the previous empirical theologians, Ritschl, Troeltsch and Harnack, who minimized the transtemporal element of the Kingdom.

The liberals of the past century were wrong, thought Schweitzer, in viewing the historical Jesus to be in error for anticipating a quick coming of the Kingdom. Hence, Schweitzer helps undermine their picture. The historical teachings of Jesus must be taken seriously, he felt, for they apply to the interim to which believers belong here and now.

Beneath the particulars of Schweitzer's theology is his philosophical principle known as "reverence for life" or respect for all forms of life, since they, too, desire and struggle to live. There is a certain individualism in this, hence Western men must overcome "mass ideas" or be doomed.

Furthermore, we must ask this: If Jesus was mistaken about the Kingdom's immanence, could he not have been mistaken about his future role as the Messiah-Son? This is not directly answered by Schweitzer but somewhat indirectly in his mystical view. This, in turn, concedes that we do not know Christ "after the flesh." Karl Barth would be apt to support this or find it supporting his position.

Schweitzer believed that the Lord's Supper left us with an important problem. The two earlier Gospels do not include a command to repeat it, the others do. Why, then, did the disciples repeat its observance save for a special significance? Why was it adopted by the primitive church if not a command by Jesus to repeat it? Schweitzer sees its repetition as a celebration associated with the expected Messianic feast in the Kingdom, which is soon to appear, eschatologically.

In addition to his famous *Quest For The Historical Jesus* referred to above Schweitzer wrote *The Mystery of the Kingdom of God,* also *The Mysticism of Paul.* In philosophy he wrote the noted work *The Philosophy of Civilization* and biographically he wrote *Out of My Life And Thought.*

Albert Schweitzer's most significant theological contribution was his eschatological jolt to the theological world, that of retaining the much neglected place for the Messianic Christ and Son of God, whose Kingdom was yet to come to fruition, not as an idealistic dream but as a divine fulfillment.

Schweitzer's "interim ethics" is in the main a futuristic eschatology, which has its faults. C. H. Dodd reacted to it negatively, because he accepted only the Johanine present tense of the Kingdom's coming, whereas Schweitzer's eschatology is kept futuristic as related to the Synoptics. These extremes are not overcome until Nicholas Berdyaev's existential perspective was allowed to embrace both the present and the future aspects of the Kingdom in his bi-polar eschatology.

Section VII

The Theology of Søren Kierkegaard (1813–1855)

Strictly speaking, with a Master's Degree from the University of Copenhagen, Kierkegaard became the author of several pseudonymous books in philosophy and religious philosophy, though he dropped the use of pseudonyms in time. He died young at the age of 42. Some of his major writings include; *Either/Or, Sickness Unto Death, Fear And Trembling, Concluding Unscientific Postscript, Concept of Dread, Stages On Life's Way* and *Training In Christianity*. Kierkegaard was not so much a theologian as he was a religious philosopher who articulated many things relevant to theological undertakings. Most basic to his influence was his anti-rationalistic and more-than-empirical type of dialectics. This blended with his anti-Hegelian frame of reference while not favorable to the rising tide of empirical thinking in much 19th century theology.

Actually it was decades after his time that Kierkegaard's views became an influence. Beneath his philosophical and religious views, Kierkegaard held to an existential perspective, which was marked by an appeal to a holistic view of a person's concrete existence. Fundamental to this relatively new thinking was Kierkegaard's broader type of epistemology, which resisted the exclusiveness of reason as long held by thinkers influenced by Greek philosophy. Reason, to Kierkegaard, was only a part of what men think with, for they learn much by will and feelings also. This implied a holistic type of epistemology, which even allowed for trans-rational understanding while reserving reason's findings for a practical Kantian philosophy, which allows for a more varied, relative and less stilted type of thought. The main reason for this is that existence, marked by everyday life, is not fully understood by reason's one-sided authoritarian view of things. The concrete self is individualistic and not to be subsumed under a rationalistic concept of man. Since human existence is steeped in much that involves choices and decisions, the will must be respected as essential to the self and often prior to reason's claims. Many decisions must be made before there is a rational security or idealistic understanding of things.

Basic to Søren Kierkegaard's theology was Christ, the sublime paradox of the God-man. Basic to his Socratic ethics that looked into "the mirror of God's Word" was "the leap of faith" which was fundamental, first, to Kierkegaard's soteriology and, second, to the consequential respect for Christ's teaching as centered in love. Spiritually, any form of religious conformity was not deemed acceptable. Essential to true Christian faith was the encounter with the Word in "the moment," which re-orients a sinner's life. Overcoming "the abyss" between the finite man and the infinite God, "the leap of faith" which entails a person's total life, makes for the "absolute relationship with the Absolute."

The Moment of faith commitment opens up the relevance of a Grace-revealed divine transcendence, which surpasses any form of religious immanence. Beneath every decision essential to our concrete existence, Kierkegaard maintained, is an *enter/eller* or either/or of commitment, which resists any form of conformity. "The crowd is untruth," he declared. It is a demoralizing pressure, hence one's role-playing "masks" must be removed. While idealistic and even religious conformity are inadequate they are often supported by the Hegelian System and subordinate systems which obscure the dialectical issues, tensions and decisions of existence. These often give rise to the paradoxes of thought and life. The paradox is "unthinkable," Søren Kierkegaard asserted, yet life and love must persistently think it, since they are more than reason.

Rationalistic views of religion and ethics fail to address the concrete conditions of the self. Hence, Kierkegaard emphasized "the teleological suspension of the ethical," as reflected in Abraham's decision to sacrifice Isaac at God's behest. A test of faith, this sort of decisiveness was not arrived at by a Hegelian rationalism or any other pre-fabricated idealism. "The particular is higher than the universal," said Søren Kierkegaard. Rationalistic theories do not address "me" in "my" condition. The subjective perspective of the individual is more basic than the objective concept of man. "Subjectivity is truth," said Kierkegaard. One cannot elude or evade the subject-self. Only the subject can think or choose or know. The self must not merely reason his way to life's answers but choose. An anxiety-laden condition this is basic to finding one's true selfhood. "Who am I? What am I here for." and "Where am I headed? are inner questions for which a person seeks answers, lest be succumb to "sickness unto death." The realistic despair or *Angst* which results from the latter uncertainties can be good in the sense that they open up the "leap of faith," a total-self commitment.

The tensions of thought boil-down to the paradoxes of existence. Eventually, only the Paradox of Christ can address and re-direct these ambiguities. Despite the goodness of a moral sensitivity, such as supported by Kant, man has an evil propensity, as Kant even conceded. Kierkegaard saw the answer to this in the transcendent theology for which Kant groped with respect but to which he did not clearly subscribe, philosophically. Søren Kierkegaard came to believe in "self-transcendence" but not merely in his own consciousness and conscience but in the higher Transcendent Self who encounters him in the Moment. In relation to his existential despair consequential to finitude, Søren Kierkegaard said, "I am transcended." He saw this through Christ to be related to the biblical "I Am." The Gospel of John stresses this.

In the face of the tensions of existence Søren Kierkegaard shrewdly said, "Not to choose is still a choice." He also said, "I must choose myself." Even if one comes to despair, he said, ". . . so then choose despair," for it is not to be ignored. Socrates said, "Know thyself," but since will is more basic to the self than reason, Kierkegaard said, "Choose thyself." Self-fulfillment is not a rational matter but a holistic self-commitment,—but to what? It is a faith commitment to the Christ-revealed Yahwah, the great "I AM," and this opens up the greatest fellowship of spirits ever known, even as it discloses one's true self to oneself. The focal point of faith is God who is "Being as such," the "I Am" who yields "the purity of heart," the pure freedom of which is "to will one thing," the good as disclosed by Christ. Such faith as "total-self commitment" is the antidote to despair and the basis for true freedom as it looks to the Unconditioned or the revealed God and his moral principles. Apart from this a person is not clear to himself or has not found his "eternal validity" or true selfhood. One's "eternal consciousness" answers to his existential yearning for authentic existence. It is linked with harmony with eternal being, thus "only before God is a man his true self," said Kierkegaard.

One of Kierkegaard's strongest contributions was his version of eschatology. What he referred to as "the Moment" was also an encounter of eternity with time. With a special precedent in the incarnate Christ, time and eternity were held by Kierkegaard to be distinguishable, yet interrelated. Since they mark the difference between the transcendentally infinite and the temporally immanent or the divine and the human, they are dynamically related in "the Moment" of faith as focused on "Christ our eternal contemporary." The meeting of time and eternity in the spirit of the faith-conditioned believer is another type of subjectivity. It makes for what is sometimes called "existential time" or what to Søren Kierkegaard is eternity "reflected" in time, a somewhat Platonic view. This is identified in the New Testament as *kairos,* which is a moment of *chronos* i.e. common, historic time, modified qualitatively by the eternal in the faith-conditioned Moment. This makes otherwise common time truly uncommon with potentialities that exceed ordinary history. The special dimension of *kairos* opens up a special quality as the present moment looks to the future fulfillment of time as "the moment is perpetually affirmed." Basic, then, is not what theory of objectified time may be held but what is the *meaning* of time, especially *now* for the person of faith. Here is the existing self who is eternal but existing temporally. In it the abyss is bridged through the divine Christ who comes to us before we come to him.

Section VIII

The Theology of William Temple
(1881–1944)

William Temple was the Archbishop of Canterbury, who was special-ized in philosophy and was an active leader in social ethics, ecumenic-ity and the World Council of Churches.

Temple became quite creative as a theologian as he combined Platonic idealism with orthodox doctrine. As such he brought up to date the theology of the medieval church in Augustine's train. In so doing he also helped bridge the gap between scientific determinism and revealed truth; also between miracles and a personal God.

Temple had an empirical approach to religious experience, which blended well with the scientific method while related to given doc-trines. Cosmically, Temple saw all reality having a divine mind, will and purpose immanently within it. In this respect he saw Mind and Idea as prior to material reality while giving order and meaning to all reality, a Platonic perspective. Temple in this context saw the Logos doctrine as a New Testament adaptation from Greek philosophy, which gave credence to the orderliness of the universe and the laws of nature while also as the Johanine Word reflected in Christ. In this regard Temple espoused a blend of creation and revelation. Though the Incarnation was mystery it was also a metaphysical clue to the structure of the universe, he held. Thus philosophy and theology are seen to meet in Christ on the basis of the Logos being not only a metaphysical principle but an event-person as well.

These views and many implicit elaborations thereof were presented in Temple's greatest work, *Nature, Man and God,* which was well received as a series in the famous Gifford Lectures. He was also the author of other prominent works including *The Faith and Modern*

Thought; also *Christian Faith and Life* as well as *Christianity and Social Order.*

In general natural theology as based on philosophical arguments was seen by Temple to blend with revelation as based upon the above contentions. The classical view erred in seeing these two types of thought to be different in method. Temple viewed them both empirically; therefore, natural and revealed theologies were two sides of the same coin. Thus the modern theologian must look to the Bible and the Church for both types of thought, Temple believed. This was a new note of emphasis.

Basically, nature reflects an order governed by intelligence. This principle amounts to an introduction to religion even as it gives support to man's trust in a personal God. Yet natural theology alone cannot point to an object worthy of worship, Temple conceded. Only the revelation of a personal God can do so. Such a God is holy and transcendent as a Person while immanent in creation as well. On this basis God can reveal himself through creation while not fully identified with it.

Temple disagrees with some popular notions such as the idea held by many scientists that the laws of nature are universal and unbreakable. For him there is room for miracle, which is a disruption at times or a discontinuity within continuity. This view favors divine transcendence somewhat like mind over matter while akin to discontinuity as a matter of degree, also to the relationship between mind and body allowing for both continuity and discontinuity.

For Temple all divine activity is revelatory, lest a deism set in leaving the world on its own save for some divine intervention. Ultimate reality, however, is distinctively different, since it is not only the ground for all else but is personal as Spirit. General revelation, Temple maintains, is essential to special revelation, it is the created order as used for revelation and redemptive purposes. This is something which Karl Barth, the neo-Reformed theologian, disagrees with, since to him revealed truth completely surpasses empirical and rationalistic thought, there being a discontinuity between reason and revelation. But for Temple all existence reflects God, so he sees a rational basis even for special revelation. Various events may be interpreted as tributary to revelation, so there is a mental dimension to this relationship as well as to revelation per se. God is apprehended, then, in revelation, because man is *imago dei,* whose reason and conscience have some continuity or kinship with ultimate principles. The Logos is "light unto every man," while supremely so in the Son of God.

The Incarnation remains a mystery, says Temple, while it is not Kenotic. It is supernatural, the idea of the historical Jesus being inadequate, since it is too temporal as an anthropological view. The Messiah-Christ, after all, is the bringer of the Kingdom as divine transcendence works through what is historically and humanly immanent. Redemption centers in Love, not judgment, while being a love which supercedes human loves like Eros and Philia, since it is Agape or self-giving, sacrificial Loves. (Interpolated under the influence of Nygren, the Swedish theologian specialized in classical and Christian understandings of love.) The Cross and atonement imply a costly love because of God's righteousness. The latter must judge, but love, nevertheless, forgives.

Popularly, Temple's theology was overshadowed by the onset of the neo-Reformed or neo-orthodox emphases of Barth and others with its down-playing of reason, which includes Temple's claim that empirical findings are in harmony with revelation. Is this view changing today? If so, why and how? Can Temple be an intermediary here? Does he offer a legitimate or necessary correlation of creation and redemptive revelation? Has neo-Reformed theology possibly passed over a problem here, or has it defected all accommodations to reason of which Temple's Platonic scheme may be one? How do Temple and Tillich compare at this point? Each seeks to communicate theology with philosophy. How are they alike? How different? These dialectical issues need to be confronted by the theologians of today.

Questions arise like the following: Why should there be a need for a special revelation if based on a theistic rational order already understandable to men? Can reason apprehend God? What about the Divine Other beyond or in relation to the infractions of finitude? Has Temple sufficiently conceded a discontinuity between reason and revelation, whatever their continuity? These questions are essential to the dialectics of contemporaneous theology and religious philosophy and may prove pertinent to the thought of the next century.

Section IX

The Theology of Karl Barth
(1886–1968)

Karl Barth was a Swiss Reformed clergyman who had close associations with Goettingen, Munster and Basle. He became a most controversial and prominent theologian of the early decades of the twentieth century as he promoted a reactionary Neo-Reformed or neo-orthodox movement.

Under the constraints of World War I Barth saw the inadequacies of the liberal theology of his day. Reacting thereto in 1918 he wrote *Die Romerbrief* or *Commentary on the Epistle to the Romans*. This scholarly book was a most influential provocative work, which was quite revolutionary in theological circles. It was a reaction against both Scholastic or natural theology and the modern empirical theologies of previous generations while in favor of complete divine transcendence.

In short, Barth stressed that man cannot know God through his ideas and systems of reason. This reactionary position was fomented under Kierkegaard's influence. God as the Wholly Other was deemed the Holy Other, who must break in upon man's consciousness. God saves man's souls from the world of time, not within it. Man is under the constant "yes/no" dialectic of God's judgment and Grace. All that belongs to evil, sin, death and hell is not of God's good creation but that to which God always says "No." This implies human competition and disjunction from God. Hence, man is under a permanent spiritual *crisis,* for creation is by the miracle of Grace with which man is in competition.

Faith to Barth is a God-given response to God's Word. Not a product of reason it is a given knowledge and salvation. Social action, consequently, does not bring in the Kingdom, a matter which caused many churchmen to label Barth a pessimist. The church was regarded by Barth as a means for spreading the Word rather than an end. This view was held to blend with the dichotomy of human understanding and the Word. Man's activism was no substitute for a redeeming Grace.

The Word is found through the Scriptures as a "living" message which must confront men to convict them of sin and point them to the Grace of the Redeemer-God. The Bible is not about a rational world but speaks of events of revelation in which God acts, uniquely invading human life in the incarnate Christ. Preaching must witness to this *kerygma* and not echo modern secular thought. By it man is removed from his pinnacle of self-sufficiency under the sovereign will and power of God as *Agape* (self-giving Love) in action. On this basis the New Testament is the new covenant *in* Christ, not just of or about him. Christ is the act of God as the God-revealer and is far more than the historical Jesus as empirically perceived.

Much in Barth's first great work on Romans was quite negative, but in time he moved away from this negative emphasis. But in deflating man's egocentric disposition Barth was anticipating man's true hope. The parallel in Kierkegaard was the despair, which led to man's submission to God. Barth's evangelical emphasis on Grace was a positive type which actually carried within it a universalism of salvation. God wins out over all things in the end. Cf. his book, *The Knowledge of God And the Service of God,* a Gifford lectureship. Here Barth is strongly dialectical but proves to be a theologian of the revealed Word. He has returned to the Reformers under Kierkegaard's impact with fresh insights that begin to shake the Protestant world, while also gaining respect from several Roman Catholic scholars. Later, however, Barth tried to drop Kierkegaard's existential ideas.

The Word of God also means "the Word made flesh," for Christ is the self-expression of God. He is the true *imago dei,* what we were meant to be but are not. We are restored only in Him, who has conquered sin and death, which are *now behind* us. Not really pessimistic, Barth means that man finds his real selfhood in Christ by living by faith under Grace. This is a hopeful assurance and joyous proclamation. Critically, however, Barth does little to relate this regeneration to our culture.

Barth is viewed to be irrational by some, but he is so only in the sense of being trans-rational, since he says man can know God solely by faith through his act of revelation in Christ. The question remains: How are we obliged to think about this systematically and ethically?

The strong result of faith is that men are not morally impotent when committed to the Word in faith and obedience.

Sin is known in terms of what Christ forgives. Election is not the old notion of the elect versus the reprobates but, positively, that all are elect in Christ, who is the truly elect one with whom one's faith identifies him. Christ assumes the burden of sin and guilt for all men and overcomes what otherwise would be their reprobation. All men are of the elect, but not all men know it. The Gospel gives them the good news, the kerygma proclaiming God-in-Christ.

Like many thinkers, Barth passed through periods of thought. He was first a so-called liberal associated with the "social gospel" movement under the state church. This movement was led by Schleiermacher and Ritschl before World War I. Barth came to see a higher need than empiricism could offer. Yet he was always sensitive to sin based on man's desire for independence. In 1918 when he published his *Commentary on Romans* Barth became more dialectical as he came to respect transcendence over immanence. In this respect he turned against liberal subjectivism with its blending of man and God. Now influenced by Kierkegaard he saw certain disjunctions between man and God. In the second edition of his *Commentary on Romans* Barth referred overtly to the "infinite qualitative disjunction" and so much as said that man should stop trying to be as God. He said, let God be God on his transcendent terms.

Also, Barth declared that we must be confronted by and crucified with Christ, the Son. The Cross of atoning Grace is where the Holy and the sinful meet. Here selfish pride is judged. It was even religious men who crucified Christ. Yet divine Grace removes our rags of righteousness and re-clothes us in the robe of divine righteousness, which gives us a new status here and now. (A problem arises here: How is the subjective condition of men affected? Barth seems indifferent to this.) The cross-centered atonement implies nothing meritorious. Justification by faith is basic here, but it yields no "new heart" inwardly, only a new status from the new relation with God. Thus sanctification is doctrinally snubbed.

Here we see where the dialectics of opposites stands out. The "Yes" and "No" appear as the Holy versus the sinful; the Creator versus the creative; Grace versus judgment. All forms of self-willing by man receives a "No" from God. (Cf. his essay entitled "Nein!") Important is what God thinks of man, not what man thinks of God. God invades history in Christ, who, as Kierkegaard declared, is "our eternal contemporary." God encounters men in his Word. (This implies the *I and Thou* held by Buber.) Barth protests any claim to a continuity between God and man. Contrary to Hegel, Schleirmacher and Ritschl and more in common with Bultmann, Brunner and Gogarten, Barth views revelation as incomprehensible. Christ is not limited to past history but speaks from the Word in the present.

Christian faith, then, is due to the impact of the Divine Other and the God-given response to the Word. This implies an objective relationship from the Godward perspective. Barth tried to retain this rather than make Jesus a modern idol or idealistic hero of sorts. Barth's theology of the Word is consistently to be seen in this light. Accordingly his work *Christian Dogmatics* or *Die Kirkliche Dogmatik* with its several volumes was an attempt to declare a systematic biblical theology of the Word. Higher criticism was not forsaken but no longer in the hands of the modernistic Jesus of history people with their type of idealism. Yet Bultmann became a stronger example of this.

Barth in his *Dogmatik* increasingly from volume to volume came to where he dropped idealistic categories and existential language together with the dialectics of time and eternity as influenced by Kierkegaard. Christ was for Barth the Word who is true God and true man in one Person. In his later works Barth declared that the only *real* time is God's time. But could he have come to these points without the pangs of his earlier stages of thought? Hardly. Critically, did Barth eventually become more *or* less communicative? It seems less so, because transcendence is beyond the empirical and temporal thought forms.

Turning now to Barth's doctrinal highlights a few of the most basic may be stressed. (a) The Triune Godhead is fundamental. (b) Christ's Incarnation is closely related. Yet here Barth leans toward a Nestorian position within the dual mystery. Christ is God as well as *fleshly* man. (c) The Church is important while catholic ecumenically as the Body of Christ. It is the steward of the Word and sacraments whereby men participate in the death and resurrection of Christ. (d) Regeneration follows as the new creaturehood, which is a qualitative dimension of the union between God and man. This relates to personal salvation as well as the social, political workaday world and its orientations. (e) The risen Christ is still at the Father's hand spelling hope for men. The Church need not despair, since He has conquered the world and it will not come to corruption. (f) The Church must not live in the past but in the present and its present assurance putting on daily the appropriate forms of its new life as given and received by faith. This new life is the leaven of the Kingdom. The Church is not its own end. She must proclaim the saving Kerygma (proclamation) to all men. (g) Grace-triumphs in creation, election, reconciliation and eschatology. Man as created is not eternal, for his time ends. Does this end belong to a good creation? Yes and no. Death is not a neutral or normal return to the "not-being" from which we came. It is rather a return to God. Linked with sin and judgment the return is not "natural" immortality. The "empirical end" is not the same as the "natural end," it is the end of man's "untruthful" or distorted existence. Sin is an alien power, as St. Paul contended, and death "came by sin." As such death is a sign of judgment. But Christ's death sheds light here, he having undergone it for us. By it judgment has been executed and borne by him.

Barth does not infer a general immortality similar to the Greek theory. Rather, at the horizon of our death is the Grace of God in Christ, which triumphs over death in his resurrection. Reconciliation is the victory of life over death and the end of time. Thus life is not prolonged after death but "eternalized," for there is no finite future related to the redeemed life. Life as it "has been" temporally in finitude is now given place in the communion with God, who lives beyond man's finitude. The resurrection of the dead expresses this. True, God determined by creation that man should have a temporal end, but the empirical fact of death makes it more than a matter of a good creation. Hope is in co-existence with God while not merely in being freed from finitude. All creation ends when its divine purpose is fulfilled. While not a temporal continuation, this is still an eternal preservation that is supra-temporal. So, to God nothing is lost. God is ever together with his creatures and they present with Him. Reconciled, a life "having been" is now glorified; it is a qualitatively superior form of life, since above time through the Christ-fulfilled triumph over sin and death in the Eschaton.

Reflections on Barth's theology have aroused such questions as the following: Is Barth too other-worldly? If so, how, why and to what consequence? Is he communicative or too one-sided for that? Does he take liberties with language and philosophical vocabulary? In his later years Barth managed to take history more seriously as related to an eventful Incarnation. This in turn, seems to account for his qualification of his original stand in *Die Romerbrief.* He has given man a larger place in the divine-human encounter, partly because he must recognize what he calls the "humanity of God" as brought out in *Die Menschlichkeit Gottes.* Also, one sees signs of it in his later volumes of *Die Kirchliche Dogmatik,* where he articulates a more dynamic concept of eternity, even though the only real time is that which belongs to God.

Barth seems to have recognized that a redeemer-God can hardly be immune to either the problems or conditions of his own creation as he relates himself redemptively to a fallen, sinful man. Toward his later years we began to wonder whether Barth would move toward a more Brunner-like point-of-contact? If so, to what extent? We also wonder how far Barth would go with his evangelical universalism. Grace is extended to every man, whether he realizes it or not. Is it not inevitable that all should be saved, then, by the God who is Agape? If not, it should have been necessary for Barth to allow a greater place for man's freedom than he had done hitherto.

Many thinkers became appreciative of Barth's revolutionary swing of the pendulum with its fresh clarification of the divinely transcendent as the ''Totally Other.'' Among them were several American theologians, who came to be more ''realistic'' in their outlook on the sinfulness of man and the need for a stronger view of redemption than the other rational, liberal and empirical appeals had warranted. Reinhold Niebuhr, Edwin Lewis, Walter Horton, George Richards, Nels Ferre, Wilhelm Pauck and Carl Michalson were among them. Lewis and Horton, however, retained a profound respect for the empirical element such as brought into prominence in America in the 1920's through the work of men like Rudolf Otto and D. C. Macintosh. ''True, God is 'the Wholly Other,' but he is not therefore 'the Wholly Different,' '' said Lewis. This qualification is correlative to God being not only redeemer but also creator, something Barth's neo-orthodoxy for a long while failed to take seriously. Creation, too, is the act and Word of God, providing the media between minds and spirits in a world of symbols. Lewis declared, if God speaks it is because man can hear Him, and if God incarnates Himself it is because man is ''the vehicle'' of the revelation. Thus, while the revelation is of God's transcendent Word, Grace and willful initiative, it is, subordinately, an experience to man, whereby God imparts His truth upon giving man a role in that impartation. Sinful as he is, man is salvageable, since addressable, by God. Barth had failed to allow for this point-of-contact with man. Brunner kept it alive without a natural theology.

Other notable books by Karl Barth include *The Word of God and the Word of Man; Credo; Against The Stream; Dogmatics in Outline; The Church and War.*

Section X

The Theology of Emil Brunner
(1889–1966)

From Zurich, this Swiss dialectical theologian had a broader neo-Reformation emphasis. Brunner was quite creative but largely in reaction to Barth's more consistently transcendent theology. He, too, had a theology of the Word, but let it speak more to the human situation via human thought forms.

Brunner allows for *das Anknüpfungspunkt,* the point-of-contact between man and God, contrary to Barth, while also accentuating man's deficiencies of sin and finitude, together with the primacy of Grace and the Incarnate Christ. He was fearless respecting Biblical criticism in the face of the *Kerygma* and the Word with the Christ of faith being primary. He was not in favor of the complete otherness of God. He held to general revelation, but not natural theology, finding it through nature and man's conscience. But this does not save; it only guides and condemns. In it, however, is a latent evangelical form of universalism, quite like that of Barth. Nels Ferre came close to Brunner here.

Faith *involves* the self subjectively, but yields a new Grace-wrought relationship which is also objective. Reason knows only phenomenal knowledge (Kant). Cf. Barth. It cannot penetrate or grasp the Ultimate, let alone the God who is Person-Subject who reveals himself. The Holy Spirit inspires us from within, unlike Barth's claim of no human involvement. By Grace we are new creatures in Christ. But the *Imago dei* is more humanly substantive than in Barth. It is marred by sin, but not destroyed. (Barth sees it more as a communion restored in the True Image of Christ). Brunner, too, but has preserved the point-of-contact ontologically this way and has seen even fallen man as a distinctive being with potentialities realized under Grace.

The Bible is the Word as the living Christ confronts the reader in the Spirit. It is a record of Divine-human encounters thru which the Word is conveyed even as by them it emerged, though supremely, in the Son-of-God.

Christ is the Divine Mediator, but it is not substantiated by the miracles or the Virgin Birth. Also, he is more than the historical Jesus of reason's empirical perception. He is God present in the Now.

Brunner had a more communicative theology than Barth, since man has a broader role in his salvation. He combines dogmatics with forms of apologetics in a "missionary interest." He wants to apply the message of the Church to problems confronting modern men, especially when not disposed to accept the Gospel. This calls for more of an inductive approach showing the superiority of the Gospel and its clues to human problems. Barth says: This is the revelation of our salvation; Brunner says: Here is the human problem, and this is the Gospel's answer to it. Barth has more of a *dogmatic* witness; Brunner more of a concerned witness. (Note the room for an existential perspective in the latter, which it seems Barth largely dropped in later years.) Brunner wants a Gospel which proves relevant today. Barth, too, but almost as if his approach "didn't care" about relevance. Brunner wants to cross-fertilize between the gospel and contemporary thought, whereas Barth sees nothing in common to allow it. (Is Barth fearful of secular accommodations in another form? Is he right or safe in this respect? Safe but not right, perhaps?) What have Brunner and Tillich in common here? Bultmann? Has Brunner demonstrated his point in going to Japan for instance? What of writing his *Eternal Hope* after his son died?

Brunner recovers the insights of Reformation theologies. These include divine sovereignty; the sinful condition of man (an existential view of the Fall rather than the old orthodox biological corruption); and justification by faith. He has the same truth of the Word but with different forms for today. He is opposed to the post-Reformation, Protestant scholastic systems as too static. The historic credal versions of the Trinity likewise, due to rational formalizing of a more dynamic, flexible New Testament doctrine. Reformation doctrine is basically sound, though later versions are confusing. But 19th century modern theologies watered down these doctrines due to too much kinship between the natural man and God, also with nature and the cosmos. Both Hegelian and empirical forms are wrong, as Barth also averred.

Theology needs perennial adjustments in form, and it needs always to be corrected by the Scriptures but not uncritically. There is no set, final form thereof. To claim so is a rational desire and ambition, which makes static the dynamic Word addressed to each person. It is an artificial claim.

The Bible is more than a religious anthology and more than a collection of revealed propositions, though containing the latter in the witness to Christ. It contains a message, which is the Word and which is the self-disclosure of God in Christ, who must be encountered by faith.

Like Barth, Brunner sees the doctrine of Christ as central to all others. This is asserted in *The Mediator: his Dogmatics,* too. We must see all doctrines thru the basic truth: God was in Christ. Christ is God's Word (Logos and message). He is what God says and does. He is the Divine Act of redemption, yet He is God incognito (cf. Søren Kierkegaard and Barth), for not all who look at Jesus see the Son or the Father. We need more than an historical Jesus-idealized.

Truth is always an encounter. Cf. *Divine-Human Encounter.* Theologians are often slow to see this in the Bible. Not a subject-object antithesis on a rational basis, it is an I-Thou relation. Old orthodoxies both Roman and Protestant, objectified it; liberal empiricisms subjectified it. Both are wrong. (No either/or here!) An object calls for a subject to perceive it, yet cannot in ultimacy. (Cf. Kant). We cannot combine the noumenal and phenomenal. Revelation is not creed but God Himself as exposed to man. We must not impose a system of thought on this. Sin is a rebellion of which an imposed system is an intellectual form.

The sinner is still responsible to God. Grace is the initiative, but this does not mean man is passive. (Contrast Barth) The Bible speaks of neither God nor man in themselves but in relation. Here is a personal correspondence of spirits. The Lord must be known to be truly Lord, so is not the same Lord over sub-human species. The initiative is not man's, contrary to Pelagian, idealistic, mystical and pantheistic or humanistic versions of man and God. Man is dependent and yet independent, God's "other" as a person. So all total determinisms, Augustinian and others, are out. But true freedom is redemptive; it is a completely willed dependence on God at His bidding, judgment and inspiration. Here Brunner protects the more persuasive aspect of the call. (Actually, it is Arminian but commonly overlooked as such.)

Faith is not mere *credo* but *pistis* or trust. Justification is not to be regarded as the forensic idea found in Paul or Luther. Faith also "completes" atonement, i.e. it is not fulfilled until relevant to the "me" of faith, existentially.

The Incarnate Word entered history but was not a part of it, since based in eternity. Brunner here sees the faith factor indifferent to anything in common history. (But did not God use it in a man Jesus, we ask, by whom the Word came and was, in part, personified and acted out?) This is also related to Bultmann, Barth and others today. (Is eternity oblivious to time and history? If so, how can it give them meaning or be concerned about them?) Contrast Ritschl and Harnack here.

To Emil Brunner the Virgin birth and bodily resurrection are not fundamental to the Gospel. The New Testament speaks of the risen and living Christ, who is a believer's privilege to trust; not the unbeliever's for whom there is no Risen Lord but only a man of Galilee and a cross, objectively speaking. The Risen Lord is to be encountered. Cf. Paul's experience. (Is this a spiritual resurrection? If so, what is that? Resurrection must involve the whole man, not just the body.) The problem at least humbles us respecting the form of its claim. The strength of Brunner's view, Bultmann's too, is that it is less vulnerable to rational attack, since only faith can accept it. Historicizing the witness to it and objectifying it is a form of rationalization, which demands that it be accepted as sheer fact to anyone, especially when the body is stressed as if it were essentially the same as before, say, scientifically. There is a mystery here regardless, but this view so much as says you need not make it appear ''preposterous'' in a sense of the natural order of life and death being altogether defied. There is a higher aspect to it than is objectively perceptible; it calls for a spiritual perceptibility of the encounter and is known only in that encounter. It makes not the least sense apart from encountering Him, who is the Eternal Word. (Yet, we say, the bodily change cannot be negated unless you reduce the event to sheer myth or symbol. Something unique happened, yet its meaning ''to me'' is prior in significance to its ''happenedness.'' This shows it is more than a historical event.) *Historie* does not proffer men this; only a *Heilsgeschichte* made relevant by faith's encounter can. To keep it sheer history invites a rational attack and obliteration. (Yet, for the believer is it an either/or proposition? Is it a both/and synthesis? If so, Hegel is right! Is it what I call a both/and tension bespeaking a paradox of interrelation but not synthesis? I say there is no such thing as an either/or paradox, even ethically, save as the alternative is a decision, both sides of which must be relevant lest there be no choice!)

Man In Revolt is Brunner's discourse upon man and his problem of sin. Written four years before Reinhold Niebuhr's *Nature And Destiny of Man* and from which Niebuhr drew heavily without conceding it in writing! Not that Niebuhr was not creative, but that he got much help from Brunner. (Note: Niebuhr was primarily an ethicist adapting theological views of Barth and Brunner to ethical problems anthropologically and socially. He saw need to reorient the "social ethics" of the American twenties. H. Richard Niebuhr and Edwin Lewis also saw the need as early as around 1930.)

Walter Rauschenbusch crystallized much of the ethical problem socially in America, but followers were prone to debilitate his evangelical basis; however, Rauschenbusch himself re-wrote his theology to "conform" with his social ethics. It was from this trend that the Niebuhrs and Lewis withdrew.

Brunner has an existential version of the Fall. The Imago Dei is restored in Christ, while he is not as clear cut about this as Barth has been, since Brunner has had an interest in the point-of-contact making it a more difficult thing to handle and a less revolutionary regeneration since more akin to man's psychological nature. For Brunner the existential wholeness of man is involved while the Spirit addresses the whole self to renew it and restore the imago dei.

The Theology of Rudolf Bultmann (1884–1976)

Rudolf Bultmann was a professor of theology at Breslau and Giessen; also in the New Testament and early Church history at Marburg for 30 years. He was a pioneer in Formgeschichte.

Bultmann combines the *Kerygma* with the form criticism of the New Testament writings and the existential perspective of the encounter. He is best understood from the standpoint of grace and justification by faith; the Kerygma or its message is basic to this.

Bultmann's approach was influenced by Heidegger's view of the cruciality of the present tense of existence, already there is the need to choose (Kierkegaard). You must decide in the face of imminent death and your *Dasein* (being there) as related to the moment of faith.

The New Testament message is not based on scientific fact and history and need not be; it is an interpretation of faith with a witness to it. History is always an interpretation of events. It is more like *Geschichte* than *Historie*. The New Testament is neither an objective record book nor a summary of dogmatics. It has sundry forms of witness including mythological types. Yet the Kerygma is witnessed via existential faith portraits in the New Testament.

So we have the primacy of the "Christ of faith" over the Jesus of history, who cannot be legitimately objectified rationally. Messianic consciousness is a historical datum for the intellect. Christ as the Word of God in the encounter is a faith factor, which is not based in history but in eternity. Yet, faith, not reason, sees Christ was God humanly manifested, "as the paradox" of the Word-made-flesh.

Central is neither the event (object), nor interpreter (subject) but their existential meeting now (for meaning). Worship is in the living present, not the dead past. But the New Testament witness includes irrelevant forms like antiquated cosmology, but the Word is not identical to them, so it can be relevant now, if you de-mythologize (de-literalize and de-historicize) the scriptures. Rudolf Bultmann would say Jesus is historical, but you cannot say the Incarnation and Resurrection are; they are not empirical matters amenable to objective (historical) reason but faith, existentially. Revelation is related to history but is not history per se since supra-historical, which includes the subjective side of relevance. (Contrast Barth on the latter point.)

Revelation is the saving event, (Heilsgeschichte), a meeting of eternity and Geschichte. Jesus does not save; Christ as the living Word does. This is an eschatological matter based on eternity and the end. We are not dependent upon the dead past; salvation is from a sinful past; hence, the inadequacy of a rational dependence on history. It's the eschatological event of God's redemptive act that saves, it calls for a present encounter; history is too relative. (Contrast Ritschl's appeal to history; both views have two sides, while stressing opposite poles. Ritschl's value judgment is a subjective faith, which Bultmann's is, too, but the latter is a balanced existential subjective relevance, not just an appraisal of history.)

But, is there a biblical past amenable to the historian? Yes, but the Kerygma is not of this. It is a present truth and elicits a faith commitment; history does not. The Bible brings the Word into the present regardless of the historical forms, while we must not confuse its message with those thought forms which are obsolete. The New Testament uses much *mythos* in its forms of witness, e.g. birth narratives, cosmology, eschatological categories when temporalized are not essential, lest men be bound. Why de-mythologize, then? To keep faith primary and not dependent upon lesser historical categories. The Kerygma is the eternal kernel; mythos consists of temporal husks. Mythical pictures express the meaning of Jesus as eternity's agent of the Word; they are not to be repudiated but understood as part of the writer's Begrifflichkeit and finitude within contemporary religious culture. Myth attempts to point men to origins and purposes transcending history; what they give witness to saves and gives meaning to their and our existence. Unlike the older 19th c. liberals, Bultmann does not toss out but clarifies the place of mythological factors. We must interpret them, even as today they are interpretations. We need parallels in the pulpit to make the gospel relevant today. (But can the New Testament be treated as hermeneutically as when we preach?)

Bultmann maintains that to dogmatize what is mythological and historically related thereto is to reduce the Bible and its Word to meaninglessness. (e.g. heaven "above" and similar spatial ideas: also angels and the Virgin birth, irrespective of modern science and its Weltanschauung). We need a Begrifflichkeit for our own age and minds. Divine truth is not tied down to antiquated forms. Doctrines made dependent thereupon are reduced to absurdity and repulse men of today. They must be relevant "to me" as Søren Kierkegaard said, to be truly true! Relevance entails 20th century ways of thinking the thought.

The existential perspective of man in his Dasein of concrete existence as a whole self helps methodologically to overcome difficulties here. But does it refract the Word in another way? Bultmann replies: Note the Bible's own diversity of interpretations or thought forms including conflicting mythological concepts. This approach respects mythopoetic language; sees faith beyond credal propositions. The Kerygma is basic; forms of witness and theology are secondary in kindling faith. This overcomes liberalism's proclivity to eliminate both the mythical factors and fundamentalism's face-value attitude and literalism. Bultmann wants men to distinguish form from substance in the New Testament and its theology, while there is need for both as in preaching.

But is Bultmann in danger of obscuring the cosmic, historic eventfulness of Christ? He would say "No, just keeping it in its place." The meaning for "me" is what matters. Jesus is the Savior eschatologically by whom God judges the world and men and by whose grace grants them a future with a promised Kingdom fulfilled ("reign"). We have no normative dogmatics for every generation. Cf. Brunner. The Word does not consist only of propositions. Jesus taught of the Kingdom in apocalyptic terms of a cosmic, divine irruption of the historic order; also, that the Kingdom is dawning, the divine reign is breaking thru. He did claim God's reign in himself, but it was seen that He was linked with it; Son of Man is another to come. Bultmann leans on John's emphasis on the present Kingdom of the Spirit. The early church claimed Jesus as the Messiah, the agent of the Kingdom come, while witnessing as though he were such in his terrestrial lifetime. Bultmann says, rather, Jesus is the one by whom the Word comes now and encounters men now. (Cf. Barth's Nestorian dualism).

Bultmann rejects the modern view that man is tied up with history and the natural process, as in a Greek view. The Hebrew view sees true existence in obedience to the transcendent God. Modern views reduce the gospel to utilitarian ethics. The interim ethics of Schweitzer does not solve the relation between Jesus' ethics and his eschatology and role. Bultmann says Jesus desired a radical obedience, and his teachings are valid anytime. Fulfilling God's will by faith is conditional to the Kingdom's fulfillment, though it has dawned. The Kingdom is come and to come.

What effect does this position have on the view of history? Biblically, history has a unity and goal. In contrast to the Greek cyclical view of time and culture the New Testament eschatology in Christ as the Word puts an end to profane history. (Why not redeem it, transfigure it as in Berdyaev's eschatology?) History's end is divine "breaking off", while this is also a goal. But it is not seen to come by an apocalyptic catastrophe but from within history by the Christ of the Word as the eschatological event brings the End into the present, while mainly by the witnessed Word. (But Bultmann tends to neglect the future aspect of the end as *eschaton*.)

The main paradox is that the Christian is taken out of the world, faith-wise, while living in this world; he is now in but not of the world. The Christ event and faith event belong to "salvation history." It is in eternity and happens in existential moments. (Cf. S.K. who also depreciates the place of realistic time and history saying all we need to know is that God's Son came among men, and we are his contemporaries in the faith encounter.) Thus Christian faith makes every moment eschatological; their significance is from eternity and the End therein; so we live by promise. (Cf. Barth). By Christ eternity broke time by His break into time, so believers live from the end in the present; this gives the only meaning to history. The future is open as faith looks up; hope is now.

Bultmann's works are these: *Kerygma and Myth; Essays . . . Jesus and the Word; Primitive Christianity; Theology of the New Testament,* 8 Vols. *The Presence of Eternity; Jesus Christ and Mythology; Existence and Faith.*

Section XII

The Theology of Paul Tillich (1886–1965)

Paul Tillich was a philosophical theologian of the University of Berlin, Breslau, and Union Seminary in New York, later at Harvard. He was associated with the Reformed Church.

Tillich was long deemed a "bridge-builder" between theology and contemporary philosophy and culture. He used an existential approach under the influence of Heidegger's "ontology." He sought a synthesis of correlation without sheer rationalism. He was concerned more with meaning than structure. For him the Logos and divine mystery meet in Christ, so revelation is a reasonable symbolism. Tillich endeavors to meet modern men and critics to point to the New Being in Christ. He concedes the interpreter cannot escape his own finitude and existential situation. He aims to communicate, accordingly.

Paul Tillich was less concerned about extraneous elements modifying the gospel than most of his contemporaries using the existential perspective. His method is one of correlation and address to the human condition of today. All genuine religion is based on "concern for the ultimate" meaning of one's life. One's ultimate concern is his God. Modern man has lost this "depth dimension" and must recover it; the loss is due to man's "estrangement" from Being or the ultimate, a form of Fall into inauthentic existence.

Reason and faith are correlative to Tillich. He even plays down the tension of most paradoxes of Christianity. He says reason can accept revelation; yet he rejects the supremacy of reason as an authority. Theology must address the whole, concrete man in his situation of personal and cultural crises, e.g. death and the demonic and mass ideas. The demonic is what controls men when they adhere to less than the ultimate in their estrangement from Being or God.

Tillich reflects the existential view of Søren Kierkegaard in his stress on concrete existence and its particulars versus abstract universals (like *a* man instead of the ideal Man.) Critically, however, he reflects abstractness in his own claim that God is Essence, not Existence. God to Tillich is the "ground" of all being. All finite or lesser beings are fallen and need reconciliation with Being, the Absolute essence of God.

Truth, even of the Word, matters not unless it addresses "me" or proves relevant to my situation. This implies for Tillich that "I" must apprehend it, so he protects reason here and is much less of a skeptic than Barth and Brunner who use Kantian epistemology.

Tillich sees the universe as one of order which the mind is akin to. (The Greek attitude is reflected here, the Hegelian also, since harmony with Being is desired.) But this is only possible in terms of (symbolic) revelation. Tillich appeals to Logos as the intermediary between the ultimate Essence of God and the concrete, fallen existence or the refracted being of man. (Problem: Why is not reason refracted more than conceded?) Tillich's *Systematic Theology* begins with the onto-logical pattern suggested here. (Does his ontology control his theology as an over-accommodation? It seems so.) Reason cannot know the ultimate of itself, but can "recognize" it and ask the right questions from within existence. Philosophy does this, but theology has the right answers to the matters of "ultimate concern." Philosophy is driven naturally to theology. (Cf. the experience of Nicholas Berdyaev) (In communicating has Tillich gone over to the philosophic-cultural camp to write his theology in a way parallel to Aquinas, while having a different ontology? It appears so. Yet Paul Tillich finds reason less of an authority than does Aquinas.)

The basic problem: Man's self-destroying sufficiency, despair and meaninglessness are intensified by the technological pace. There is an Abyss between being in existence and the self as it ought to be; it is reflected in art, psychology, nihilism, existentialism of Sartre, drama, politics, etc. The threat of non-being engulfs man in nothingness and dependence upon the uncontrollable powers of the age. This reflects human finitude in the face of the infinitude yearned for, unwittingly or otherwise. Existence is laden with anxiety, since any moment "I" may not be; a universal illness (Cf. Søren Kierkegaard, *"Sickness Unto Death";* also Viktor Frankl's psycho-biological existential per-spective).

Men have the need of *The Courage To Be* (title); the answer is *The New Being* (title) in Christ. The underlying temptation is the desire to be independent of the ultimate, morally, especially. Tensions of free-dom under necessities reflect the estranged being of finitude, also rebellion basic thereto as sin. Sin is a state; a separation from the Ground of being; a paralysis of will is symptomatic, also social and personal ties and the impersonalism of the crowd (Cf. Søren Kierke-gaard's comment, "The *Crowd is Untruth*." Condemnation of self and others is related also. Efforts to overcome or mask this intensify the problem, including many religious efforts. Hope begins with acknowl-edged helplessness, akin to God's despair, and the quest for "new being," the restored image in Christ, who heals the estrangement of one's finite being with Being.

Christ is true manhood unseparated from the true freedom of Being. In Him salvation is a recovered freedom by reconciliation and Grace. Justification by faith is basic. This implies that you are accepted, so accept yourself! Faith is a gift. Activism is no substitute for Grace, a state of being. Reconciliation of the self should yield all other forms of reconciliation and love; by it barriers between men are broken down.

Criticism: Note how man's creatureliness or finitude seems to be the basic problem, as it occasions estrangement. Man is free in God, while God seems to need man to come into self-fulfillment, as He is Essence, the "ground of all being." Spiritual life and freedom are given ontologi-cal theory to the extent that God is not personal in Essence, only as symbol, and the Three Persons are symbolic principles of divine operations. Man is on the frontier of being and non-being; this marks his tension and finitude; yet he is aware of it, so he transcends it also as a self and has an inner yearning or "ultimate concern" for the infinite and ultimate. This is part of the existential situation of every man. Christ represents essential manhood in existential manhood, the Absolute in the relative. This is seen by Tillich in terms of an Adoption-ist Christology. Also, the Cross and Resurrection are not merely objective facts or events of history but symbols of the Ultimate. Man senses he belongs to the infinite, though estranged; he desires it, though he may not know what it is or how to attain it.

The Ultimate is not really personal as Essence, yet Tillich symboli-cally attributes personality to Him (It?). Regarded as Love, this is Grace. But Tillich says God is Being; He does not *exist,* as that would be too finite a category for describing God. (Problems: How does such a God come in relation to the man Christ, if he exists—even symbolically? Answer: The Logos principle gives God a relation to finitude and what "exists" (as I see it). But is the Logos in any sense less than God?) Tillich says God is beyond existence, so we must not argue that He exists, for He *is*. This is an anti-naturalistic theology; yet what of arguing that God is or is Being? Are you not even more presumptuous, especially when you have asserted that any interpreter cannot escape his finitude and existence? How does a theologian get beyond his finite situation to peek into "the above and beyond" of Essence? If it is revelation, how so?)

An ethical dualism is allowed for by Tillich within a scheme, which I believe can be rightfully described as a panentheism, a bi-focal metaphysics within one organic whole of Being. Nels F. S. Ferre has something similar in pattern but geared much more closely to a process cosmology of a highly rational sort. (Note the universalism in both.) Transcendence and immanence are distinctive yet interrelated. Logos is the uniting factor for essence and existence, being and estranged being, infinitude and finitude. Christ is the redemptive side of this Logos principle. In him eternity and time also meet in kairos giving eschatological depth and meaning to history and time. (Here Tillich has received much help from Berdyaev, I maintain, but with minimal accreditation to the Russian convert from Communism.) There is a mystical element here without negation of chronos. It is a potential eschatological transfiguration of the world. (Niebuhr has adapted this, too, in *Faith in History*—derived from Berdyaev.)

Tillich's "belief-ful realism" enables a realistic view of culture and selfhood together with an answer and hope in religion; it is the epistemological aspect of his scheme allowing communication and ethical concern for this world. Cultural form must be invaded by the depth dimension of what is of ultimate concern and yields meaning to life. A split world, culture and selfhood are embraced only by the one Being, which is the whole. Psychoanalysis reflects the depth of the self.

Man lives on earth, not heaven, in existence, not essence (Ideal) Cf. Luther, Søren Kierkegaard, Marx, and William James. Also, self-assertion leads to self-discovery. But sheer autonomy becomes bondage. Autonomy needs theonomy to be truly free. This is not submission to either ecclesiastical or secular authorities but is spiritual freedom under Grace.

The Historical Jesus must not become an idol; yet, faith-wise He is an incarnation and the Christ. Tillich says Jesus sacrificed all that was Jesus to all that was Christ. While Tillich accepts liberalism's historical methods he does not make its mistake here. He rejects Barth's more supernatural dualism. Christianity is the final revelation only as Jesus yielded his finite existence to the infinite without stint; otherwise it is just another religion. For Tillich neither the wholly objective nor the wholly subjective has full truth. Like Barth, God's "No!" is spoken against every finite claim to finality. The Incarnation is symbolic, pointing to the Ultimate from within the finite and temporal.

Tillich hits the liberal rejection of transcendence as well as the Barthian rejection of immanence. There is no room for mediation in the latter. Paul Tillich's dialectic unites opposites until a "Yes" is reached; it is much like Hegel's dialectics here but not as a rational synthesis. (Cf. Berdyaev here who is satisfied with neither ontological dualism nor monism, total transcendence nor total immanence.) Tillich judges both a cynical realism and a utopian hope. This belongs to the Protestant principle based on justification by faith. But the 'Protestant era' cannot persist unless it breaks with any bourgeois ideology. (Cf. Berdyaev). A social ethic must spring from Agape and Kairos. Reformed theology fell short in making faith obscure love. Both Roman Catholic theology and liberal Protestantism neglected eschatology. To understand the gospel, history and culture demand the latter, for time's relation to eternity is most revealing.

The following are some of Tillich's leading works: *The Protestant Era; Shaking of the Foundations; Interpretation of History; The Religious Situation; Dynamics of Faith; Theology of Culture; Religious Situation; Systematic Theology.* 3 Vols.

Basic Bibliography

Part One

Schleiermacher, Friedrich
   (1) *Addresses on Religion to Its Cultured Despisers,* (1800) *die Reden,* New York, Harper and Bros., 1958.
   (2) *The Christian Faith* (1821) Edinburgh, T. and T. Clark, 1948.

Martensen, Hans L.
   (1) *Christian Dogmatics,* Edinburgh, T. and T. Clark, 1871, 1874.
   (2) *Kristlige Etik,* Danish, Vol. I, 1871–1878; *Christian Ethics,* Vol. 1, 1871.

Ritschl, Albrecht,
   (1) *The Christian Doctrine of Justification* and *Reconciliation,* (1870) Edinburgh, T. and T. Clark, 1900.

Troeltsch, Ernst,
   (1) *Absolutheit des Christentum,* 1909
   (2) *Christian Thought,* New York, Meridian Books, 1957.
   (3) *Social Teachings of the Christian Churches,* N.Y. Macmillan Co., 1931.

Harnack, Adolf
   (1) *What Is Christianity?* (1900) London, Williams and Norgate, 1904.
   (2) *Outline of the History Of Dogma,* Vol. I, Boston Beacon Press, 1957.
   (3) *Christianity And History,* London, Adam and Charles Black, 1896.

Part Two

Schweitzer, Albert
(1) *The Quest of the Historical Jesus,* New York, Macmillan Co.,
1950.
(2) *The Mystery Of The Kingdom of God,* New York, Macmillan
Co., 1950.
(3) *The Mysticism of Paul,* New York, Seabury Press, 1931, 1968.
(4) *The Philosophy of Civilization,* New York, Macmillan Co.,
1949.

Kierkegaard, Søren
(1) *Either/Or,* Vol. I, II.
(2) *Fear and Trembling* (and) *Sickness Unto Death* New York,
Doubleday and Co., 1955.
(3) *Training in Christianity,* Princeton University Press, 1949.
(4) *Works of Love,* Princeton University Press, 1946.
(5) *Stages of Life,* Princeton University Press, 1958.
(6) *Concluding Unscientific Postscript,* Princeton University
Press, 1944.
(7) *Journals of Kierkegaard,* ed. Bretall and Dru, New York,
Harper and Bros. 1959.

Temple, William
(1) *Nature, Man and God,* New York, Macmillan Co., 1949.
(2) *Faith and Modern Thought,* London, Macmillan, 1910–1913.
(3) *Christianity and the Social Order,* New York, Penguin Books,
1942.
(4) *Christian Faith and Life,*

Barth, Karl
(1) *Die Kirkliche Dogmatik,* Band I, II, III, IV. (Christian Dogmatics), Zurich: Ev. Verlag 1964–67. Edit. 8. Edinburg, T. and T.
Clark, 1936–62, New York, Scribner's, 1956.
(2) *Die Menchlichkeit Gottes,* Theologische Studien, Evangel-
ischer Verlag A, Zolliken—Zurich, 1956.
(3) *The Word of God and the Word of Man,* New York, Harper
Torchbooks, 1957.
(4) *Credo,* New York, Scribners, 1962.
(5) *Against the Stream,* New York, The Philosophical Library,
1954.
(6) *Dogmatics in Outline,* London, Student Christian Movement
Press, 1957.

(7) *The Knowledge of God and the Service of God,* New York, Charles Scribner, 1939.
(8) *The Epistle to the Romans,* 2nd Edition, London, Oxford University Press, 1933.
(9) *The Faith of the Church,* New York, Meridian Books, Inc., 1958.
(10) *Nein!* Munchen, C. Kaiser, 1934.

Brunner, Emil
(1) *Man in Revolt,* Philadelphia, Westminster Press, 1947.
(2) *Dogmatics,* Philadelphia, Westminster Press, 1950, 1962.
(3) *Eternal Hope,* Philadelphia, Westminster Press, 1954.
(4) *The Mediator,* Philadelphia, Westminster Press, 1947.
(4) *Nature and Grace,* Philadelphia, Westminster Press, London, G. Bles, Centenary Press, 1946.

Bultmann, Rudolf
(1) *The Kerygma and Myth,* London, S.P.C.K. 1953.
(2) *Jesus and the Word,* New York, Scribners, 1958.
(3) *Primitive Christianity,* New York, Meridian Books, 1956.
(4) *Theology of the New Testament,* 2 Vols. New York, Scribners, 1951, 1955.
(5) *The Presence of Eternity,* New York, Harper, 1957.
(6) *Jesus Christ and Mythology,* New York, Scribners, 1958.
(7) *Existence and Faith,* New York, Meridian Books, 1960.

Tillich, Paul
(1) *Systematic Theology,* 3 vols. University of Chicago Press, 1951, 1963.
(2) *The Courage to Be,* New Haven, Yale Univ. Press, 1952.
(3) *The New Being,* New York, Scribners, 1955.
(4) *The Protestant Era,* University of Chicago Press, 1957. Phoenix Books.
(5) *The Shaking of the Foundations,* New York, Scribners.
(6) *The Religious Situation,* New York, Meridian Books, 1956, 1963.
(7) *Dynamics of Faith,* New York, Harper and Row, 1957, 1958.
(8) *Theology of Culture,* New York, Oxford University Press, 1959, 1970.